invisible SOUL

Uncovering Cleveland's Underground Soul Scene

invisible SOUL

Carlo Wolff

with James O'Hare
illustrations Ron Hill

To the spirit of Cleveland's soul music

Invisible Soul
By Carlo Wolff & James O'Hare

Copyright © 2023 Carlo Wolff

Book and cover design © 2023 Act 3 LLC
Illustrations by Ron Hill © 2023 Act 3 LLC

ISBN 978-1-7331795-5-3

invisiblesoul.act3creative.com

June 2023

For more information or inquiries, contact:
Act 3 LLC | 12200 Fairhill Road, Cleveland, OH 44120
+1 216 325 7777

Published by

www.Act3Creative.com
3RD PRINTING · SEPTEMBER 2023

CONTENTS

While they never released a record, the El Deons were a fan favorite at many Cleveland night spots. They were also popular enough to inspire their own female fan club — the La Deonettes. (Photo courtesy Abdul Ghani)

Foreword | TO A SOUL KINSMAN

CARLO WOLFF IS A BRILLIANT WRITER, a fierce researcher, and a possessor of exquisitely eclectic tastes in music. I met him in the late 1980s, when I was working in my family's Christian bookstore, with a side gig as a gospel radio DJ hoping to break into the jazz world. His (then) wife was aware of me from radio, and suggested me as a source for a Cleveland Magazine piece that Carlo was writing about the local gospel music scene.

We scheduled an interview, and that first conversation about Cleveland gospel spawned other phone calls, lunches, and happy hours that were spent discussing bands and singers or books, magazines and authors. A friendship was forged pretty quickly through a mutual love of good music and good writing. I'm grateful that our bond has stayed strong through the years.

Mark David Ribbins

Sometime in the early 2010s, Carlo started mentioning a project that would spotlight a golden age of Soul and R&B music in Cleveland. There were a few voices in our local Black music community (some of them are featured in this book) who wondered openly whether this white man had the bona fides to do justice to the lush musical legacy he wanted to chronicle. However, the relationship I'd developed with Carlo gave me confidence that his approach would not be one of cultural appropriation, but that of a music journalist who truly loves and appreciates both the genre and the culture he sought to bring to print. I mean, this is a white brother who would hang at Gabe's Diplomat Lounge on East 116th Street at midnight Friday to hear Robert Lockwood Jr.!

Carlo pressed on with his fact-finding (as he does when he has passion for a cause), and shortly afterward he was on Facebook sharing black-and-white playbill treasures culled from the archives of the *Call & Post* and *Cleveland Plain Dealer*. The stories he unearthed pointed him back toward a distinguished era of Black music in our city, as well as to the positive and negative socioeconomic factors that were both backdrop and driving forces in how that entertainment field took shape. From his deep dive into Cleveland culture of days gone by comes the narrative that you hold.

Invisible Soul is Carlo Wolff's love letter to a socio-musical era in Cleveland that neither he nor I had the opportunity to fully experience. Carlo was living and working in other cities, and I was a little too young.

I was a 9-year-old boy in 1973 when our family's church (Providence Baptist) moved from a converted theater at 11918 Kinsman Road to a newly built edifice a few blocks away at 12712 Kinsman. Abbott's Barber Shop and Palmer's Record Store were our neighbors at the old building, but the

Part of the overflow crowd at the August 3, 2023 launch of Invisible Soul.
The event was hosted by Gadi Zamir at his Negative Space Gallery.

congregation's move brought two new, legendary ones. The first was Whitmore's Barbeque and all its amazing smells and tastes. The second, to the east of Whitmore's across East 128th Street, was the Kinsman Grill.

At my tender age, as I looked across from church toward the Kinsman Grill, the windows of the nightclub immediately caught my eye. Both held neon signs with flashing bulbs, and lettering that announced who would be appearing that week. Those signs were my introduction to many of the artists named in this book. Acts like Lou Ragland, Seven Miles High, Hot Chocolate, and Bell Telephunk appeared regularly on the Kinsman Grill marquee. I'd seen the newspaper ads and heard adults talk about them to the extent that the music seemed desirable, though unattainable. The Kinsman Grill stage was so close yet so far away, since it would be a dozen years before I was old enough to legally walk in and hear a performance. (Side note: By the time I was old enough to go to the Kinsman Grill, owner William "Sonny" Jones had undergone a spiritual awakening and transformed the place into a Christian nightclub called "Your Alternative.")

This book is a heartfelt journey that leads me to connect the Cleveland dots: from places I'd heard about (Leo's Casino, Gleason's, Hatlo's), to people and places I knew personally (Dunn Pearson Jr., Sonny Jones, Boddie's), and back in time to new stories that I couldn't have imagined.

There's a biblical passage where John the Apostle says about Jesus, "if all the other events in Jesus's life were written, the whole world could hardly contain the books!" The same is true of the book you're about to experience. Carlo Wolff certainly hasn't found or told all of the events of Cleveland Soul and R&B. Yet, through his loving, painstaking and respectful gathering of stories from musical elders of our city, his Invisible Soul provides a worthy retrospective.

— *Mark David Ribbins*

A Cleveland native, Ribbins is pastor of Avon Avenue Baptist Church. He was program director at 107.3 The Wave and is a consultant to numerous jazz artists and concert promoters.

Opening Act | BARING MY SOUL

SOUL MUSIC ABSORBED ME FROM a very early age. In the 1950s, I listened to sweet, often sorrowful soul as I drifted off to sleep. My special window to another world, it provided a glimpse of an otherness that I, too, felt. The rhythm and grit of first blues, and then soul, its urban descendant, moved and comforted me. The soul community sounded like one I wanted to join, and my youthful

yearning brought me as far as its front porch. Decades later, finally, I have broken down the door to complete this book. *Invisible Soul* feels destined.

I am the only child of Jews born in Germany. In an ironic twist, the maniacal ascendance of Hitler proved to be a strange matchmaker: after separately fleeing the horrors unfolding in their homeland, my parents met in Italy in the mid-1930s. They married, and thanks to the resourcefulness of relatives already in America, Kurt and Carla Wolff arrived in this country in 1939. They first settled in Dallas, where I was born.

The Southwest was home for just a short while. All I retain from a stay in Taos, New Mexico, where my father was doing research, is a mental picture of Reboy, a small dog I befriended there. Reboy is my earliest memory.

In the mid-1940s, we were on the move again when my father secured an assistant professorship of sociology at the Ohio State University. Columbus was still pretty rural, pretty small-town; Woody Hayes ruled. I drank chocolate milk

shakes at Jones Pharmacy on my way home from University School, the long-defunct progressive school I attended through 10th grade. Before the 11th grade, we were on the move again, this time to the Boston area so my father could chair the sociology department at Brandeis University in suburban Waltham.

No matter my childhood home, the same three words labeled me: solitary, sheltered, and spoiled. But I was curious, too, and a music fan from my single digits. In one form or another, music is my constant but invisible companion. Rock and roll, the bastard child of country and blues, is my contemporary, and we're both aging fast.

In 1956, two quarters got me into a theater on High Street near campus. In that cool, dark space I caught Elvis Presley and a lustworthy Debra Paget in "Love Me Tender." Watching Presley's film debut, I witnessed the commercial flowering of rock and roll. It certainly wasn't soul music, but it connected with me.

In my view, the progression goes like this: blues to rhythm and blues to soul to funk. Key players are John Lee Hooker—gloriously electrified, unlike the acoustic Delta blues oracle Robert Johnson—to B.B. and (unrelated) Albert King to James Brown, Marvin Gaye and the Temptations to the Dazz Band and Rick James and later pop-soulsters like DeBarge. It is a postwar phenomenon that coincides with the Great Migration. Soul reflects the urbanization of country music, muscled up with horns, electric guitar and a rhythm complement to a cappella/doo-wop.

I'm old enough to remember the beginning of this wonderful confluence. As I grew into adolescence, I spent nights in bed with my Bakelite AM radio under my pillow, listening to Hoyt Locke, a pioneering Black DJ on WCOL-AM. "This is Dr. Bop on the scene, with a stack of shellac and my record machine," Locke would say before spinning a 45 on its way up the "race" charts. Dr. Bop was my portal to another universe, and listening to him literally under cover made the emerging world of Black pop feel like I was in on a secret.

It took years for me to graduate from Dr. Bop to a deeper immersion in the Black music of the day. By my 19th birthday, I'd finally heard live music in a club. I caught the funky, post-bop pianist Junior Mance at the Jazz Workshop on Boylston Street in Boston. I was now hooked on live music too.

My appreciation of a wide variety of music types predated my professional criticism of it. But once I became a journalist in 1971, I had a great awakening: I could actually get paid for writing about music. As a music critic, I straddled two worlds: I was a professional fan. I believe my review of Edgar Winter's White Trash was the first rock criticism ever published in the Burlington (Vermont) *Free Press*.

If Vermont was my springboard to music criticism, my commitment deepened in Albany, New York, where I lived from 1977 to 1986. I enjoyed reviewing both locally and for *Billboard*, the music-industry trade magazine. Albany was a test market for many acts, particularly during the era of J.B. Scott's, still my favorite club after more than 40 years.

Dates by a very young U2, the slash-and-burn Pretenders, a scary Iggy Pop (with David Bowie on keyboards), the Jam (the loudest band I've ever heard in a club), a torrid Pat Benatar, pyrotechnic jazz trumpeter Maynard Ferguson, and the dashing Count Basie attest to the draw of Scott's, which closed in 1982 following a fire.

Albany was my last stop before I returned to the Midwest. Cleveland called when my then-wife got a job at the *Cleveland Plain Dealer*. My horizons and opportunities widened. In 1986, Cleveland was a major market and a must stop for musical attractions. It had a well-deserved reputation for breaking acts (Bowie, Springsteen and Roxy Music are standouts), venues of all sizes, and a powerhouse radio station in WMMS. I got plenty of work freelancing music reviews, from jazz to metal to funk. The Cleveland music scene was on fire. I basked in its glow then, and looking back, I'd like to think I stoked the fire too!

With decades of experience and countless performances under my belt, two soul shows—other than a Smokey and the Miracles fiasco—stand out: Wayne Cochran and the C.C. Riders in 1969 at the Sugar Shack, a club in downtown Boston on par with Cleveland's Leo's Casino, and James Brown in 1991 at the Front Row Theatre in the Cleveland suburb of Highland Heights. Cochran, an outrageously pompadoured white guy, was more dynamic—he strode the bar as he wailed and howled, punching holes in the ceiling to the rhythm—but Brown was his model. I wish I'd seen the Godfather of Soul in his prime instead of this gig in support of the Rocky IV film's corny, jingoistic "Living in America," Brown's last big hit.

I grew up during the formation of rock, a confluence of the blues, jazz, gospel and rockabilly. I reflexively sing along to '50s hits like "At the Hop" and "Heartbreak Hotel." But the '60s were the most musically fertile decade, when rock and roll was melodic, textured, and addressed real issues. Soul, particularly the strategically contagious Motown variant, spoke to the concerns and aspirations of the Black community by, in a sense, crossing over to the white community. The '70s, too, had their share of musical greatness.

In the '70s, I began writing record reviews, well before the era of compact disk or streaming services, for the student paper at the University of Vermont in Burlington. I eventually reviewed records for the Boston Globe and the record collectors magazine Goldmine, among other outlets.

I covered hundreds of concerts, primarily rock, even as rock itself was becoming more formulaic, narcissistic and less socially sensitive. There were memorable crossovers, like Talking Heads, a white band with a Black spine, in its epochal "Stop Making Sense" tour. That show resurrected the notion of community early rock and soul represented.

I first started work on *Invisible Soul* more than 11 years ago, when stories of a long-buried Cleveland musical scene coaxed me into acknowledging what I'd sensed as an oversight years earlier.

I had written a book called *Cleveland Rock & Roll Memories* in the mid-aughts. A mashup of anecdotes about the glory days of the Cleveland rock scene, *CRRM* was great fun to research and write, but I had the nagging feeling that I had short-shrifted the Black music of Cleveland, painting a picture of the Northeast Ohio musical scene more monochromatic than it was. I knew there was another story, one of Black music with a mainstream all its own. Some call that the Chitlin' Circuit, referencing a separate universe of Black entertainment that existed in parallel with and in contrast to the predominant white strain.

It also conjured a vibrant social scene.

A strong sense of community matters because it helps smooth out differences. Lack of community—make that loss, not lack—is the reason driving along East 105th Street and East 55th Street and Cedar Road and Woodland Avenue and Kinsman Road and Union Avenue is heartrending. Those streets used to jump 24/7. They were thriving, not failing. I missed their heyday. Many who were part of that scene, as well as others like me, want it back.

This book aims to get people talking. It may be nostalgic, but it's not an obituary. This exploration of vintage soul and funk in Cleveland's neighborhoods tracks underappreciated local groups and bands through firsthand stories. The foundation of Invisible Soul is built on more than 60

Lylah Wolff's photo captures (from left) Art Blakey, his wife Joyce and George Hendricks at a 2011 Hesitations rehearsal.

interviews with musicians who sang, played, and sweated to create Cleveland's soul scene. At times, unearthing this era felt archaeological as I sifted through archives of display ads in vintage newspapers, archives of the Cleveland Public Library and the Rock and Roll Hall of Fame and Museum, and the collections of performers and fans.

Hours scouring the web, researching performers and venues in the *Call & Post* and, to a far lesser degree, the *Plain Dealer*, gave me a feeling for an era when the Black community on the city's East Side presented—and supported—a rich musical array complete with radio backing, local record labels, even a pressing plant.

I now attest to what I had previously only sensed: Cleveland's vibrant Black musical scene was special. Information about what is now known as the University Circle area is at the heart of that soul culture. This "shadow downtown" had its own style and power that shined.

Along the way, I learned that a tangle of factors—including lousy timing, poor management, or an endemic complacency—contributed to a failure of too few of these talented musical groups and artists to blow up nationwide. Even worse, most never even were in a position to have a shot. Among the exceptions: the Dazz Band and the O'Jays. You'll find some coverage here, but in-depth chronicles of their careers deserve their own books.

Essentially, my investigation affirmed my hunch that this other musical world, a loud and proud Black one, energized Cleveland but was rarely covered in mainstream media. Part of the mission of this book is to help set the record straight by telling a Black story shot through with white participation. It's as much about race as it is about music. It's about an era 40 to 70 years ago when calls for civil rights, an end to economic inequality, and Black power tore cities apart and at the same time gave rise to music of lasting expressiveness and groove.

White audiences of that period typically followed the Beatles, the Stones, Dylan, Pink Floyd, Creedence Clearwater Revival, and other avatars of classic rock, folk and even country rock. Blacks tuned into songs by artists who recorded on a gang of local labels and major imprints such as Motown, Stax, Volt, Atlantic and Philadelphia International. And there were even crossover hits by the likes of the Supremes, the Temptations, Otis Redding, Aretha Franklin—and the O'Jays, who went national after they became Cleveland headliners. In the '60s and into the '70s, Motown hitmakers in particular appealed to Black and white alike.

Soul music was the soundtrack for civil rights. It was the voice of protest and freedom, too, from Marvin Gaye's "Inner City Blues (Make Me Wanna Holler)" to the Temptations' "Papa Was a Rolling Stone," the Impressions' "People Get Ready," and "Respect," a defiant Otis Redding hit that Aretha Franklin covered even more successfully. In confronting social issues, soul music presented a reality rarely touched on by mainstream rock.

I love soul music. And even though I despair over today's circumstances —political polarization, climate crises, violence, more guns than people, economic inequality, intransigence on gender—I look to soul music from back in the day as a restorative.

Fast-forward to today. Music styles, venues, distribution media, licensing, and technology are fundamentally different. What endures, however, is that vexing issue of figuring out how races can coexist. Racism is a global problem, but it's uniquely acute in the United States. Heated rhetoric over critical race theory, a view of history taught in college, rubs up against accounts of Black men freed from jail because they've been exonerated for crimes they didn't commit. At the same time, other Black men are unjustly accused, jailed and killed, lubricating the racist cycle once again.

This book doesn't pretend to offer sweeping remedies for the social, cultural and political dilemmas that rend this country. Its aim is more modest, though I hope that contributing to the historical record might help even the score.

Here are stories centered on the Black music scene in a Cleveland that was more neighborhoods than institutions, when its other downtown, centered around East 105th Street, had an identifiable personality, purpose, pleasures and pains. In the early to mid-1960s, those remaining few who worked and played there tell me, 105 was so alive there was hardly time to blink.

Stories of sweaty, electric times and places gone decades ago make me wish I'd been there, and I'm eager to present glimpses of a period when fissures that continue to deepen began to crack segregation. That account is complex and by no means complete.

Some might say that as a white man attempting to tell a Black story, my efforts are presumptuous, yet another manifestation of cultural colonialism. Rest assured: this book aims to enlighten, heal—and tell of another side of life.

Carlo Wolff

Abdul Ghani

WATCH

Can anyone have soul? Scan the QR code to watch a brief video excerpt to learn Ghani's views.

LAY
OF THE LAND

Jazz fans can point to Beale Street in Memphis, 18th and
Vine in Kansas City, Los Angeles' Central Avenue and New
York's 52nd Street as wellsprings of unique musical styles and
approaches. An unorganized, sprawling Cleveland was never blessed
with a single thoroughfare to namecheck its brand of soul music. Rather,
it has something much more diffuse and more difficult to pin down:
a large hub on the city's East Side that many refer to simply as "105."
Ground Zero was the intersection of East 105th Street and Euclid Avenue,
but its effects stretched for blocks in many directions. While civic boosters
have recently put forth "the Land" as cozy branding for the entire city and
region, 105—say it loud: one-oh-five—is dialed in. But just a typical
lifetime ago, one-oh-five seemed like "the Land" unto itself. With few
human guides and almost no physical remnants to show the way,
one-oh-five and the soul scene associated with it were things
I had to discover largely on my own. I became almost an
archaeologist of Cleveland's soul, looking for the
center, the key bits of cultural infrastructure
that defined its existence.

1 *Welcome to the* NEIGHBORHOOD

Music animated Cleveland's East Side during Invisible Soul's 30-year heyday. Fast-forward 50 years, and poverty, health care disparities, and technological upheaval background the area.

BETTER UNDERSTANDING OF CLEVELAND'S largely underappreciated soul music scene begins at an intersection on Cleveland's East Side. For decades, this vital section of Cleveland was known simply as 105. That is the brand, the label for the now-defunct entertainment district that radiated from East 105th Street at Euclid Avenue.

In 1920, just three decades before 105 grew into its soul scene heyday, Cleveland was a national power and the country's fifth-most-populous city. Today, Cleveland's population earns it a humbling 54th position. While the metropolitan region retains a respectable national ranking of 17th-largest, migration of jobs and lives to the South and the West has taken a toll on Cleveland's population, economy, and, yes, its soul.

While our broader financial base isn't the most healthy, thank God for our health care-based economy.

For well over a quarter-century, the region's largest health care provider has demonstrated the swagger and sustainability that has eluded sports teams and previously high-flying corporations. Cleveland Clinic boasts what is generally regarded as providing the No. 1 heart care in the world. High rankings in numerous health care specialties routinely propel it to a top 10 ranking worldwide, top five in the US. Patients from all 50 states and 136 countries travel to Cleveland for health care. As of 2022, the Clinic is the No. 2 employer in Ohio, just behind Walmart. Over 70,000 employees comprise the Clinic system. The vast majority of

medical professionals and support staff are located in the city, but a growing number populate Clinic extensions in Florida, Nevada, Toronto, London, and Abu Dhabi. Calculating the number of employees is a monumental feat. Calculating the direct and indirect economic benefits is Herculean.

Today, the East 105th Street-Euclid Avenue crossroads is the province of the Clinic, a massive, ever-expanding campus on the eastern tip of the city. Other medical providers—University Hospitals and MetroHealth—are sizable standouts.

Medicine is the lifeblood of the neighborhood now. Before the late '80s, though, small businesses, laughter, and music coursed through the vital arteries of 105. At its peak, 105 jumped to Cleveland soul music. Before that genre got its grip in the '60s, it was a hotbed of jazz, blues, and rhythm and blues.

The boundaries of 105 are St. Clair Avenue to the north, Kinsman Road to the south, East 55th Street to the west and University Circle to the east. Drive 105 to see what was one of the most musically rich sections of Cleveland. It now is one of the city's most economically bereft.

During the day, the Clinic complex is bustling. The surrounding slum is bleak by day, scary at night. The Clinic seems to grow stronger as the pulse of the old 105 weakens.

Much of Cleveland's East Side underscores the growing chasm between rich and poor, aspiration and despair, hope and depression. This needy area craves jobs, education, and money.

Save for the latest institutional building, the topography is abandoned at worst, hardscrabble at best. It's a sad, vivid mirror of Cleveland's poverty rate, at 32.7 percent second only to Detroit's among large US cities. The 2020 US Census Bureau designated Cleveland as the poorest big city in the country. It's sad that in this instance, Cleveland outranked only Detroit, its superior in several industries—like cars and soul music.

A view of Euclid Avenue from 105th Street in 1956 illustrating the vitality of the neighborhood. (courtesy Cleveland Public Library)

TRACT OF TEARS

IN CENSUS TERMINOLOGY, an incorporated city is considered a "place." Cleveland census data identifies it as a place that's undergone significant shrinkage. With a population of more than 900,000 in 1950, Cleveland seemed destined to crack 1 million by 1960. Destiny gave way to reality, however, as Cleveland never hit that population mark. The 2020 census revealed that just 368,000 souls live in Cleveland. Again reflecting parallels between the cities, Cleveland was second only to Detroit in population loss in the latest census. And within a census place are important designations called tracts, on average bounding a population of about 4,000. Tracts that include Glenville, Hough, and parts of East Cleveland rank in the highest Census population density category (more than 10,000 per square mile). But just 40 years ago, they were far denser—and more vibrant.

Roads are potholed and treacherous, houses boarded up and crumbling. Many houses are demolished annually, but not enough to outrun the decay. Natural forces sometimes intervene. Many of the homes built in Cleveland's go-go decades of the early 20th century eventually have become victims of the elements. It's as if they finally give up fighting gravity and neglect, breathe their last—and self-implode. They simply, slowly, fall down.

Gas stations, funeral homes, dollar stores, churches, and the rare bar, eatery or barbecue spot give the area what life it has. It's not contemporary, multi-investor, highly planned civic development, but at least it's something. Here, it seems, people buy most of their food at quick stops. Google Earth provides an uncomfortable birdseye view of the gap-toothed holes and weedy vacant lots where schools, homes, businesses, and entertainment venues once made 105 such a force.

Kevin Conwell is a longtime Cleveland councilman, lifelong Glenville resident, and, among other endeavors, a drummer in several local jazz and soul groups. For him, the effects of this demise are personal. His childhood neighborhood was buzzing, full of successful Black-owned businesses, doctors, dentists, lawyers, and shop owners. "I was able to walk around and see success every single day," Conwell says.

This city used to pulse 24/7, and it flourished well into the '60s. But the Hough Riots of July 1966 resulted in the death of four Blacks. Two years later, the Glenville Shootout left seven Blacks dead, providing a second blow; some might say the latter was a knock-out punch. In the aftermath, fear proved to be a powerful motivator. Both white and Black flight accelerated dramatically, as did the city's slide into penury and despair.

Not much is happening beyond the mostly gleaming realm of the Clinic, Case Western Reserve University, University Hospitals and the many other cultural bastions in University Circle. Scattered development slowly unfolds in Glenville, especially south of Superior. At the southern terminus of 105, the aspirationally named Opportunity Corridor roadway holds promise that may fulfill its proponents' assertions that it would be more than just an expensive shortcut for high-income commuters. At more than $100 million a mile, it's one of the more pricey interstate segments ever built.

Current and proposed development spurred by the Corridor provides hope for sustainable jobs, housing designed for many income levels and family styles, and further investment to re-make an area dubbed Cleveland's "Forgotten Triangle." But change comes slowly—the Corridor came to life after more than 20 years of discussion and planning, and over 50 years since a predecessor plan failed. Fits and starts is a mantra for a city that needs to move past assembly-line mindsets. Change comes especially hard and slow—or seemingly not at all—to this achingly poor part of Cleveland.

While a neighborhood and a population waits, you're confronted with a world that's limping. Paint peels off the facade of a once-proud printing firm. Trees sprout from the roof of a dead plumbing business. A lot next to a surviving mini-mart was the site of the Paddock Bar & Grill, where the great, androgynous Cleveland balladeer Jimmy Scott performed in 1953. The geography of 105 is a ghost of the music that once animated it. But it lives on, not in any clubs in that area (I have found none) but in inspiring Invisible Soul legends. These include the crack aggregation of former Hesitation Art Blakey, the blues-blaster band of Travis "Moonchild" Haddix, and Sly, Slick & Wicked, a group John Wilson founded in the '70s. Alphonso Boyd, a founder of the Imperial Wonders and a member of Truth who also wrote for Motown, shuttles among various groups in Los Angeles. The music also smolders on recordings trickling into the mainstream through archival record labels and specialty compilations.

NEW LIFE FOR OLD GROOVES

THE CLEVELAND BRAND OF soul music, strikingly nimble but also full-bodied, is long gone from radio airwaves, but it still inspires on scarce, highly prized 45s and even rarer LPs. A few performers from its salad days play the rare local club or the private social gathering. Some try to start anew, peppering legacy song lists with fresh tunes in order to reach a younger audience hungry for authenticity. Others have given up on period originals that never struck commercial gold, instead finding more reliable work as cover bands. Cleveland, home to the Rock and Roll Hall of Fame, takes pride in curating nostalgia, after all. At the same time, it also seems more supportive of the new, both in soul music's birthplace, and abroad.

Fans in the British Isles—and Japan—do their part to keep this largely up-tempo musical offshoot alive. In the U.K., Northern Soul lovers collect rare vinyl from the period, eschewing Motown for less polished, rarer stuff, primarily from America's Midwest. They dance to its heavy beats and soaring melodies at specialty clubs and present reverential concerts where performers discover a celebrity status they never knew they had.

In addition, social media are slowly rebuilding bridges between members of a musical community that reached its zenith decades ago. Facebook, Twitter and YouTube link former 105 players to fans old and new, virtually restarting bands that dissolved in the distant past.

Shake, Rattle & SOUL

Theaters, clubs, after-hours joints and a unique cast of characters made Cleveland's "uptown downtown" a magnet for musicians and fans of all colors.

AT ITS PEAK, 105 WAS NOT ONLY A PLACE where entertainers made a living. It was also a place where they had fun by bringing such joy to their fans. Invisible Soul venues ran the gamut in size, style, and sophistication, and in Cleveland, they were concentrated in the East Side. Most large US cities in southern, eastern and upper Midwest states had similar concentrations of Black entertainment and performance venues. From the 1920s through the 1960s, stifling segregation practices steered Black audiences, performers, and club owners to seek safety in shared proximity. A similar social scenario played out at about the same time with another cultural group.

The New York Jewish community—performers, vacationers, hospitality owners—congregated in about 500 clubs in an upstate region called the Borscht Belt. Named for the beetroot staple familiar to many eastern European immigrants, Jews found community in an era when they, too, faced a lack of understanding at best, distrust and violence at worst.

The safe space for Blacks was called the "Chitlin' Circuit," referencing chitterlings—pig intestines—that were an unsavory food for slaves. Over time, Blacks acquired a taste for chitlins as it became a cultural comfort food. In a similar fashion, the Chitlin' Circuit served as a comfort space for Blacks during segregation.

Cleveland's Chitlin' Circuit mainstays included the Circle Theatre, the Chatterbox, the Red Carpet Lounge, even the cavernous, drafty Cleveland Arena. The area just west of University Circle was its core, but joints also jumped along Cedar Road, Woodland Avenue, Central Avenue, Kinsman Road, even west to Public Square. Savvy, hustling musicians could work their way to early morning through clubs and theaters all down the line.

INSIDE THE CIRCLE

CONSIDER MANNY STUTZ'S 1,975-SEAT CIRCLE Theatre. In the early '50s, when the Cleveland music scene never slept, the Circle Theatre was a special magnet, according to Kaye Friedman, whose husband booked shows there. In those youthful days of rock and roll, the Circle, at 10208 Euclid, was just one of five traditional theaters in 105. Stars who performed there included Ray Charles, LaVern Baker, and Chuck Berry. "That's where they should have built the hall of fame because that's where it all happened," claimed Friedman, who died in January 2023.

Her spouse, Sidney "Syd" Friedman, was a Cleveland promoter who booked acts into the Circle. Friedman clients were typically soul acts, but Syd also presented the transgressive gay singer Johnnie Ray and the novelty act Tons of Fun, four women whose combined weight totaled more than 1,000 pounds. Among other acts he managed: the early doo-wop group the Hornets, and the Wigs (with a young Art Blakey), colonially attired Blacks touted as the "black Beatles," mobilized to fight the British Invasion. The office for Friedman's All-Star Theatrical Agency was in the Hippodrome, an 11-story building at 720 Euclid that was torn down in 1972. Syd died in November 2003, after making quite a mark on Cleveland's soul scene, even if he and the Wigs never did stand much of a chance in winning that battle against the Beatles.

According to Kaye Friedman, each Circle Theatre engagement included up to five shows a day, each show about an hour-and-a-half in length. Demand was high; she said lines stretched around the block for a big draw like Loretta Mary Aiken. Better known as Moms Mabley, Aiken was an irreverent, risque vaudeville favorite reputed to be the first female stand-up comedian. Other Circle standouts included the comedy team of Charlie & Ray and exotic dancers Takeela Davis and the ubiquitous Estelle "Caldonia" Young, who was known as the "grandmother of show business."

Try this actual show lineup: on September 29, 1957 the dazzling singer Jackie Wilson, packing "Reet Petite" and "Lonely Teardrops"; Otis Williams and the Charms; bluesman Nappy Brown; Hammond B-3 organ stylist Doc Bagby; the vocalist Annie Laurie; and the Buddy Lucas Orchestra. The emcee was Charles Eckstein, the "added attraction" a group called the Five Dreams. Syd Friedman promised four shows that day starting at 2 p.m., "with a movie thrown in

Kaye Friedman, in concert with her husband Syd, was a prominent promoter of Cleveland's soul scene.

for good measure at the end of each stage show," according to a newspaper preview from the day before. Quality and quantity entertainment, served daily at the Circle.

Tickets to the show Domino headlined, also featuring the Drifters, cost $1.50. More value on 105.

The Circle Theatre, best-known for hosting Elvis Presley's first appearance north of the Mason-Dixon line in February 1955, closed in 1959 and was demolished shortly thereafter. Its former site is now occupied by the Crile Building, the signature structure of the Cleveland Clinic and its center for outpatient services.

Working the Circle was fun, said Friedman, and she and Syd felt comfortable there—for the most part. "It was scary at times," she said. "We had all that money on us at the end of the night." Since this was in the pre-Mastercard and Visa era, all that money meant "all that cash." It's said that cash is king, but it sometimes shows up as the devil, as it did to a legendary blind singer who on at least one occasion was shorted by a promoter.

"Ray Charles wouldn't go on one night until he got his money before he did the show. That was a problem. We usually paid them at the end of the night," Friedman recalled. Since promoters often relied on fat concession revenue during the performance, especially intermission, Friedman was in a pinch. If the show didn't go on soon, the Friedmans were fearful of a riot. Somehow, Charles got his money and another notable soul performance in Cleveland was in the books.

The Friedmans were among the few white couples to frequent Black clubs, trawling for talent they could present at bigger venues. During the mid-50s, the couple also frequented the Majestic Hotel at 55th and Central, the premier lodging spot for Black entertainers. "They couldn't stay at just any hotel so the acts would stay there," said the widow Friedman.

In the Majestic's Rose Room, pianist Duke Jenkins led a band, and Caldonia presented talent.

"Caldonia used to bring all the acts there who wanted to get bookings. She had a talent night there, a kind of showcase. That's where Syd would get a lot of his acts," Kaye says.

As a result, many more lucrative stages were open to Black acts, an unintended but often positive consequence of Invisible Soul-era segregation practices, at least for the performers.

RACE RELATING

AS THE DEMOGRAPHICS OF Cleveland's Chitlin' Circuit and especially 105 evolved, music created a tenuous bridge between whites and Blacks. Tom Baker, a classically trained white musician known for his arrangements and production work, effectively led the house band at a premiere club for integrated audiences.

Baker grew up around East 152nd Street and St. Clair Avenue. At Collinwood High School he played jazz trumpet but switched to bass guitar after falling under the spell of Motown legend James Jamerson. The band Baker eventually led included an integrated collection of Invisible Soul virtuosos: saxophonist Ernie Krivda, drummer Val Kent, and guitarist Lou Ragland. Another regular was trombonist Fred Wheatt, like Ragland a Black. The others were white.

It would be false to proclaim the arrangement as idyllic. In fact, the scene could be edgy.

"I'm going to tell you exactly how it was," says Baker, who arranged music for groups spanning the Outsiders (of "Time Won't Let Me" fame) and the O'Jays. "I'd walk into the bar, guys would say, 'You white motherfucker!' Walking through those bars, I would be terrified. You

I'D WALK INTO THE BAR, GUYS WOULD SAY, 'YOU WHITE MOTHERFUCKER!'

don't know what's going to happen any second."

On his way to the stage, Black musicians seemed skeptical, but "after I'd play with them and go back through the bar, the same guys who were screaming in the beginning would go, 'Yeah, bro, yeah. You play nice.' What a crazy scene."

Music can divide, but quality musical talent can unite or at least defuse racial tension.

The scene in the '60s and '70s was a busy, lucrative one, especially for artists flexible enough to perform with all kinds of bands. Motivation and hustle resulted in nice paydays.

Bars used to close from 2:30 to 5:30 a.m., giving entertainers time to refuel. For example, a vocalist could start the evening at Liz Fredrickson's Liz's Lounge on 105, go to the Continental at 127th and St. Clair, then wind up at the Round Table, an after-hours joint at 83rd and Quincy.

In the 1960s, typical earnings might be $25 a show for a vocalist, same as band members, and there were at least two shows a night. In perspective, $25 was a lot of money in 1960, equal in buying power to almost 10 times that in today's dollars, adjusted for inflation. Not a fortune, but not a bad evening's work for performers doing what they love.

Abdul Ghani, formerly known as Eddie Williams, began his career as a member of a doo-wop group called the El Deons. It seems their primary wage was fun: El Deons gigs were all for free, he says, though they may have gotten some "payment" in the form of clothing that might double as stage attire. And of course, it's not possible to place a dollar value on being the center attention of the ladies in the audience, eager to catch the eye of a dashing El Deon.

Talented entertainers could make a decent living, but they had to keep a relentless performance pace.

You could actually make a living entertaining in those days. You had to be good, though.

SOUL TRACING, BY THE NUMBERS

THE CLUBS THAT ONCE PULSED with entertainment are almost all gone. Same goes for the storied studios, though the sign for the Boddie Recording Company remains. The abandoned site of Way Out Studios, on East 55th Street just north of Chester Avenue, is forlorn and desolate. Any tangible mark of Saru Records, at East 140th Street and Miles Road, has vanished, taken over by a grassy plot next to a small church.

The survival of signs like Boddie's and a neon beauty atop Jack's Tavern on Cedar Road at 68th are visible outliers. Leo's is now the site of an Aldi supermarket; a commemorative plaque that once marked the spot went missing in civic archives for years following a redevelopment. One commemorative plaque, sponsored by the Rock and Roll Hall of Fame, still stands at 78th and Cedar to mark where Don King's Corner Tavern once rocked.

King, a Cleveland native, is best known as a boxing promoter.

In the late 1990s, King shifted his enterprise to become owner and publisher of the *Call & Post*, Cleveland's long-running Black newspaper. But before that career move, and before King arranged multi-million-dollar deals with networks, brands, and brawlers, he was a bar owner.

Back in the days of the Corner Tavern, he was also known for running the illegal betting operation that was the precursor to state lottery games, including the Ohio Lottery. The numbers game, as it was called, was an integral, if dangerous, part of the lifeblood of 105.

At its heart, the numbers game was simple, retail gambling. Every day, one winning number from zero to 999 was a winner. The best-run games used a simple formula from published data (e.g. stock market closing values or the numbers of horses that won specific races at specified tracks) that was hard to rig. Bet a dollar and if your number comes in, you win $500. The other $500 covered overhead: the agent, who might be the shop foreman, a bar owner, the corner druggist, or a neighbor, got a cut. The person who collected money and aggregated bets (and others who might do the same) would get increasingly lucrative percentages.

Mostly, the game worked. As little as 50 cents bought a few hours of hope or as much as a few months' apartment rent (and a round or two at the local tavern) if your number hit. Local money stayed mostly local, flowing through the neighborhood.

But the numbers racket worked best for those who operated it, particularly those operators who were willing to be brutal.

Violent, often deadly situations unfolded daily, mostly in large Eastern and Midwestern cities, over turf, ego, and, of course, money. A runner who collected bet slips might one day decide to not turn in some of the slips or the cash. And if one of those numbers hits that day, angry bettors and suspicious racketeers could mean a runner with a broken arm—or worse.

A detailed Wikipedia entry on the topic indicates that the numbers racket in Cleveland was among the most expansive, innovative—and brutal. Runaway profits (aided by protection money paid to police and judges) led to new schemes, new intimidations, and sometimes lurid murders.

The numbers game was woven into the fabric of inner-city Cleveland and its soul scene. Its cash flow often provided a steady, tax-free revenue stream that could help small business owners weather rainy days. Numbers money could even fund entrepreneurial ventures.

Word is that street-gambling profits provided the foundation for Way Out Records, a label launched by numbers figures Lester Johnson and Red Thompson, along with Cleveland policeman Billy Branch. According to Don George, an influential record promotion man, Johnson was an "old numbers guy who supposedly went straight," and Thompson was Don King's "numbers guy."

The numbers also dogged Wilbur Dean, who with his wife owned Dean's House of Jazz, a chain of four record stores and a "one-stop" wholesale outlet where other retailers could buy records. The IRS identified the Deans' operation as something else.

In April 1965, IRS agents descended on their residence, seizing three adding machines and three Buicks. They alleged Dean used his Wade Park home as a "bank" and "count house" for a numbers operation. Key haul: $305,000, the largest numbers grab to date. That May, in what some suggested to the *Call & Post* was a numbers war, a "mystery blaze" destroyed the Corner Tavern. A year earlier, a House of Jazz store was dynamited. Talk about a combustible operation.

It took 20 people four hours to count the Dean cache—51 bundles of $5,000 each, according to contemporary newspaper accounts. That November 29, the IRS smacked Dean and his wife Delores with a $755,000 tax lien. The case played out for years.

The attorney representing Dean was James Willis. He also represented King, adult entertainment entrepreneur, jazz impresario and gambler Winston Willis (who owned various clubs and businesses along 105th Street from the late '60s to the early '80s) and Shondor Birns, a notorious mobster who owned the Alhambra, a popular entertainment outlet at 10309 Euclid. The Alhambra housed the Red Carpet Lounge, a hot spot in the late '60s showcasing local talent like the Sensations and Phyllis Haynes, a singer with the Jimmy Landers Trio, who later foreswore soul for gospel.

Birns died in a car bombing in 1975. Attorney Willis suggested that as a major numbers operator, Birns kept peace among lesser numbers lights like Dean and Winston Willis (no relation to the lawyer).

BEYOND THE NUMBERS

WINSTON WILLIS WAS CONTROVERSIAL, an entrepreneur who in the '70s and early '80s owned 28 properties, mostly along Euclid Avenue. These included Big Daddy's Equipment Company, Winston's New Orleans Restaurant, and the Scrumpty Dump theater.

IT TOOK 20 PEOPLE FOUR HOURS TO COUNT THE $305,000 FROM THE COUNT HOUSE

According to a 2017 article on medium.com, the footprint of Willis's University Circle Properties Development was not only an affront to some prone to racist leaning, it was a threat to organizations like University Hospitals the Cleveland Clinic, and Case Western Reserve University. All three wanted to create a dominant medical-educational district that needed to include the Willis territory. Eventually, the manifest destiny of the "eds and meds" prevailed and prospered.

At his peak, Willis had close to 25 businesses, employing more than 400 people. But none of Willis' many ventures survived.

The environment of this era suggests that 105 was an ambiguous, contradictory web, nothing if not fluid. From the '50s to the '80s, it was a cultural hub. It also was a gray area, as much a state of mind as geography.

The action wasn't confined to 105th and Euclid, however. Go a few blocks south of Euclid to Cedar Avenue and a little west to Central and you would find another string of clubs, including Gleason's Musical Bar, and Leo's, before it burned down in 1962 and quickly reopened at 75th and Euclid. Gleason's and the original Leo's are lots vacant except for For Sale signs.

Call & Post display ads used to bulge with entertainment activity. In a single week in December 1961, these ads proclaimed, Sam Cooke and Chubby Checker worked the Pla-Mor Ballroom (aka Pla-Mor Roller Rink) at 10626 Cedar; the Three Sounds and Ramsey Lewis played Leo's (then at 4805-4817 Central), and the blues singer Amos Milburn was featured at Gleason's at 5219 Woodland, up the street from Leo's. Blind saxophonist Roland Kirk was performing at Club 100, at 10020 Euclid, with Eddie Baccus Sr., Cleveland's Hammond B-3 legend, then on piano.

The spill of names can be bewildering, but the bigger picture is clear: activity along 105 was so heated, the most diehard music lover would have been hard-pressed to keep up.

IN THE THICK OF IT

105 WAS FUN, BUT it wasn't exactly stable. Then again, perhaps that constant shifting of music, performers, venues, and audience is what made it so special.

Affirming that flux are people who effectively lived all over 105, like singer George Hendricks and guitarist-vocalist Harvey Hall of Harvey and the Phenomenals, veteran showmen who became fast friends. Working the same Chitlin' Circuit, sometimes in the same band, brings people close.

Even the determinedly sunny Hendricks admits the good times could be challenging.

In 1969, he recalls, Black nationalists took over the Merry Widow Bar at 2026 East 105th in an attempt to clean up the neighborhood by preventing prostitutes from using that bar as a base. Police positioned themselves on rooftops across from the bar as a precautionary measure.

Liz Fredrickson, who at various times also ran Liz's Lounge and the nearby Esquire Lounge at 10530 Euclid, was pressed into peacemaker mode, entering the Merry Widow to negotiate with the nationalists, and quickly pacified the situation. As Hendricks says, the area effectively policed itself.

In the late '50s, Hendricks was a smooth, skinny teen-ager, up with the latest fashions and styles. He certainly got around—and to hear him tell it, fooled around. Today, he's a heavier, greyer family man, sidelined by a stroke in 2016. Until then, he was on his way back as an entertainer, working with old friend Art Blakey in a revival of the Hesitations, a popular soul group of

A member of the "Mayor Committee" helps restore a storefront damaged in the Glenville neighborhood in 1968. (Cleveland Public Library)

the late '60s. When I met him toward the end of 2010, he still dressed dapper. Sang dapper, too. Hendricks was hot in the 1960s.

Like Hendricks, his old friend Hall also rounded out over time. In the late '60s and '70s, when his Phenomenals were at their peak, he was a compact, mustachioed style-setter, perched on a stool while cradling his guitar like a baby. His approach to the guitar remained, but in the second decade of the 21st century, Hall customarily wore a porkpie hat and moved a little slower, and where there used to be uniforms, there was business casual. Things slowed down for Hall, but he never lost his sense of rhythm, his low-key, entrancing showmanship, and his joy supporting his wife Etta, a strong, sassy vocalist. Hall died of COVID-19 complications in January 2022.

A DOWNWARD SPIRAL

IN A 2011 INTERVIEW, Hall deplored how times, like the neighborhoods, had changed for the worse. Despite the racial stress that boiled over so grievously in 1960s Hough and Glenville, there was always work, and Hall landed his fair share.

A minimalist, funky guitarist and singer, Hall in the 2000s led the Magic Touch Band, featuring Miss Etta on vocals. Before he was the "Harvey" of Harvey and the Phenomenals, a snappy rhythm 'n' blues outfit that played original material, Hall led the doo-wop group the Fabulous Five Flames. Like Hendricks, he was a professional musician for more than 60 years.

All these groups and solo artists knew each other, often following one another into the same nightclub.

There was competition, sure, but also pride and joy. There were "cutting contests"—a performance competition between groups with the audience determining the winner. Hendricks remembers going up against the mighty Futuretones when he was a member of the Sahibs—and plenty of work for all.

Hendricks shakes his head at the memories. Those were good times, wild times, bawdy times. A standout gig took place in the early '70s in the Native Son, a club at Kinsman Road and 153rd Street. Hendricks was working with Lou Ragland and the guitarist Eugene Ross in The Chosen Few. It was Halloween night. In his recollection, he could swear the Temptations dropped in.

There are a few remnants of that scene, clubs where soul musicians still perform occasionally: Joe's House of the Blues in Euclid, and The Beachland Ballroom and Tavern in Collinwood have mounted several soul shows.

It wasn't always so sparse. There used to be so many places to play. Hall recalled those good times fondly, even though racism tainted his memories.

In the '60s, Blacks rarely ventured east of Collinwood beyond Five Points, where 152nd and Ivanhoe streets meet St. Clair Avenue, he said. Farther east, along St. Clair to 216th, was a Middle European neighborhood. Like Little Italy east of University Circle, it was hostile to Blacks, in Hall's view.

Urban renewal killed 105, decimating the small businesses that peppered the East Side, Hall said, calling Section 8 housing the worst thing that ever happened to a neighborhood. Hall said it ruined Slavic Village, a neighborhood that became known nationally as a poster child for the foreclosure crisis.

Not that times were easy then, when Cleveland was much bigger and economically far healthier. But they were eventful, and they could be dangerous.

NO REST FOR THE WICKED

HALL RECALLED A NIGHT when he was 18 or 19, performing with his Fabulous Flames in Silks Café at 3101 Scoville Avenue off East 33rd Street.

Hall's group was under age, but Silks was a neighborhood bar; such establishments usually looked the other way. A fight broke out when a Flame began fooling around with someone's girl "and her man came in and they got to tussling," said Hall. The boyfriend pulled out a pistol and began shooting at the Flames, hitting Hall in the lower abdomen. He recovered at Mount Sinai Hospital. Silks is long gone. So is Mount Sinai.

Well into the '90s, Hall worked three or four nights a week, earning enough to afford a car, pay rent and outfit himself. After the clubs dried up, he went to work as a restaurant supply salesman. He finished his career working part-time for the railroad.

Most of Hall's musical scene is gone, but until very recently, he still performed. And some 12 years ago, he licensed Harvey and the Phenomenals material to Numero Group, the Chicago label specializing in unearthing, documenting and then promoting obscure music scenes.

Hall liked Cleveland. He also despaired for Cleveland. "I've seen it go from sugar to shit," Hall said years ago. "You just try to survive the best you can."

I'VE SEEN IT GO FROM SUGAR TO SHIT. YOU JUST TRY TO SURVIVE THE BEST YOU CAN.

3 REVIVING
Cleveland's Soul

Cleveland soul music provided the rhythm of hope, much of which sprang from prospects for real change from the administration of a promising, progressive mayor. That political era was also fraught and frustrating, and despair set in again. The soundtrack of that time lives on in veteran performers, fond memories, and admirers of Northern Soul worldwide.

IT WAS WARM, AUGUST SHADING INTO September. The scene was a party for Carl Stokes, making his first run for mayor of Cleveland, Ohio. The band wore black pants and black-and-red tuxedo jackets. The dance floor was full of suits and high heels, though the mood was far from formal. A new era of politics was on the rise, and Chuck and the Tremblers were there to get the party going.

The year was 1965. Tonight's bash at an East Side club was full of energy and high hopes.

Travis Haddix, the Tremblers' guitarist and vocalist, remembers the vibe of the gig, held at the now-defunct Riviera Country Club on Solon Road.

Haddix was 25, and he and the Tremblers had one job that evening: get folks moving. They did, too. The candidate and his wife, Shirley Stokes, did some high stepping. Carl Stokes was, among other things, a fine dancer.

Haddix has a faded Polaroid from that night, showing Carl and Shirley in front of the band. The picture is a memento dear to him, as is the memory of playing his crying, sax-drenched blues song, "Stop Cheating Woman."

The Tremblers played "Duke of Earl," too, Gene Chandler's majestic soul tune. The beat went on, the melodies rose and fell, and the crowd let loose. Like the politics of the period, the music surged with memories of dark times and hopes for something brighter. Blues was turning into rhythm and blues, sometimes hinting at soul. Uptempo tunes gave the crowd to the Jitterbug. Sleepier songs brought on the Slow Drag.

Optimism was in the air, Haddix says. "Everybody was upbeat. We thought that Stokes was going to win the election. Everybody was really, really happy."

Stokes lost narrowly in 1965 to incumbent Ralph Locher. But a mere two years later, he beat Locher in the primary and then won over Republican Seth Taft. Chuck and the Tremblers had played their first important gig just as Carl Stokes's career was about to flower.

The same could be said for Cleveland soul music. Over the course of some 20 years, it blossomed, briefly flourished, then faded. But in its heyday, Cleveland soul—raw, sweet, funky—bubbled under everything from family gatherings to risque entertainment. The background of great parties like Stokes's, Cleveland soul shook dance floors and provided a soundtrack for a social network that continues to resonate.

UP TO THE MAIN FLOOR

THIS JOURNEY BEGAN THE evening of January 4, 2011, when my daughter Lylah Rose and I pulled into a driveway in Maple Heights, the Cleveland suburb where George and Irma Hendricks lived. Hendricks had invited us to his home for a rehearsal by the Hesitations.

A favorite of Northern Soul fans who like its fervent blend of gospel and pop in such late-60s hits as "Born Free" and "The Impossible Dream," the Hesitations hadn't performed in a Cleveland club in decades. Hesitations II was formed by founding member Art Blakey, like Hendricks a former Sahib.

Lylah and I went to the Hendricks home to preview the first Hesitations show in a Cleveland club in decades. The group was scheduled to play the Beachland Ballroom, Cleveland's signature music venue, that January 22. It would be their first gig since they drew some 4,000 to the Northern and Modern Soul Weekender in Prestatyn, North Wales in March 2010. Their most recent Cleveland date was in 2006 at the Rock and Roll Hall of Fame.

When the Beachland publicist contacted me about writing a preview, I jumped at the chance. I figured the four vocalists and five instrumentalists in the Hesitations would have great stories to tell. I also assumed they would sing and play well, and they'd surely be genuine.

Past and present coalesced in the Hendricks basement that night as Old School experts and their young band tried revival on for size.

Travis Haddix and his band rocked Nighttown until COVID came to town.

A BASEMENT SNAPSHOT

THE GROUP RAN THROUGH its signature tunes, mid-tempo songs that speak to the aspiration soul music

expressed even as the optimistic '60s curdled into the '70s. They resurrected Carla Thomas's sweetly querulous "Gee Whiz," and Blakey and his wife, Joyce, harmonized on "She Won't Come Back," a stirring track from the Hesitations' Soul Superman album. Hendricks and Blakey traded vocals on Wilson Pickett's bawdy "Mustang Sally," goofing with each other.

Cut to a couple of weeks later, when a snowstorm hobbled the Beachland date, resulting in a draw of only about 150, most of them friends and family. The show was fine anyway. The Hesitations powered through hits from their salad days—the standouts were "Soul Superman," "Born Free" and "The Impossible Dream"—and knocked out a nifty, reggaefied "Stand by Me" and a winking "Mustang Sally."

Another Beachland date that June 4 drew better. The group was looser, yet more polished. At the start of 2012, The Hesitations were working on their first album since 1968. As an appetizer, it re-recorded Luther Vandross's "Dance With My Father," which even got some airplay.

All seemed to be aligning for the Hesitations as the group continued to plug away, performing in Cleveland clubs and writing new material for a planned album. But everything ground to a halt in January 2016, when Hendricks suffered a stroke, rendering him incapable of performing.

The Hesitations died a second time. Now, only Blakey powers on as head of the Day Nites, a crack younger group that helps this "Soul Superman" stay up to date.

TRAVIS TRIUMPHANT

A SOULMAN WHO HAS not only survived but prevailed is Travis "Moonchild" Haddix, who began as a rhythm and blues player. He's a renowned guitarist and singer at home in various styles who until the pandemic toured Europe regularly and still makes his living from music.

Lining his basement walls are pictures of Haddix with various European blues stars. One frame contains a record instead of a photo. It's a copy of "Stop Cheating Woman/ Dianna," a single recorded by Chuck and the Tremblers, the group Haddix played with when he came out of the service in 1965. It's on the Del-Nita label, which was owned by the Rev. John B. Hicks, a gospel fan who strayed into rhythm and blues from time to time. It was recorded at the Boddie operation on Union Avenue. That 45 tells multi-leveled stories, suggesting Chuck and the Tremblers had some mighty times.

Back in the Tremblers day, teen-aged boys eager to sing would polish their act on the street and at school dances. In black-and-white photos from this binary era, their faces are upturned beneath a streetlight, mouths open in heavenly harmony. The topic was girls, the mode was yearning, and the beat was implied in the vocal arrangement.

But there is another, less familiar and less guileless image from this world parallel to the mainstream. Incubated by racism, doo-wop became rhythm and blues, funk and soul, the musical backbone of a thriving scene. Black entertainers engaged Black audiences with music, dancing, theatrics, and comedy. They performed in their own clubs, stayed in their own hotels, advertised in their own media, and ate in their own restaurants.

Music, however, was always the bridge. Black musicians worked with white musicians. The failure of a white-owned record pressing plant led directly to the success of one owned and operated by Blacks. A white band called the Originals made its name doing Motown covers. What some call one

IF CLEVELAND HAD A CHAMPION LIKE BERRY GORDY, COULD SOUL MAGIC HAVE BEEN MADE HERE?

of the greatest funk songs of all is Wild Cherry's "Play That Funky Music," a top hit in 1976. Wild Cherry was white. At the same time, a key house band in Cleveland's most famous club was white—except for its multi-talented guitarist.

The music made along 105, earlier known as Doan's Corners, stretched into the '80s and beyond through groups like the O'Jays, the Dazz Band, and Levert.

The O'Jays came into their own at Leo's, where even '90s superstar Gerald Levert, the son of lead O'Jay Eddie Levert, took his baby steps. The club was such a magnet, color didn't matter—until the Hough Riots of 1966 persuaded the National Guard to end a Supremes show and send the audience home. Cleveland soul music, hidden for far too long, was waxed at long-defunct enterprises like Hicks Recording, Boddie, Way Out, the more mainstream Cleveland Recording, and the Saru label. The pressings were tiny, the distribution spotty, the labels ephemeral and obscure.

I wish I'd caught the great soul singers Kim Tolliver and Edwin Starr; jazz sax men Joe Alexander and William "Weasel" Parker; Duke Jenkins, leader of the Majestic Hotel Orchestra; and Dewey Jeffries, the pianist who gave jazz singer Vanessa Rubin her start. They, too, were in the Invisible Soul weave.

As catchy as Motown but less formulaic, Cleveland soul failed to reach the mainstream, but not for lack of talent or creativity. Perhaps that's because there was no Berry Gordy in Cleveland, no mercenary visionary to push the music. Blame lack of a champion. Blame lack of management. Blame groups for not being hungry enough or too satisfied with their local status. Whatever the reason, soul and funk in what was then Ohio's largest city were too fragmented to brand, break out, and make a concerted national splash.

THE FOUNDATION OF CLEVELAND'S SOUL

It is no coincidence that the glory days of Cleveland soul music overlapped much of the city's postwar heyday, particularly the 1950s and '60s. Fueled by escapees from the segregated South, the Great Migration that defined much of America's 20th century led to robust population growth and a booming, industrially based economy. While the economy, that scene, and the city itself literally "went south" in the '70s, a few vestiges of the institutions and sounds that made Cleveland such a magnetic and memorable place can still be found. One of the most storied and beloved of those institutions was a farm-to-table operation known as Boddie.

The Wonders of
BODDIE WORLD

Boddie Recording Company was a one-stop shop for musicians of all complexions and genres. It was a quintessentially local company with a long and deep reach. While it could have spread its wings to even greater height, Boddie's flight was inspirational.

DRIVE WEST ON KINSMAN ROAD IN Cleveland past the car dealerships and the big car wash and the neighborhood turns rough and lonely too damn quick. Small bargain stores and Chinese takeouts dot Kinsman, and for the brave outsider, gas is cheap here. Around East 140th Street, Kinsman splits from Union Avenue, and business dries up, giving way to the occasional small church and clapboard houses. Drive a few blocks farther west and many of the houses are boarded up, falling down, or gone. Such are the tears in what 60 years ago was a healthier city fabric. Just past the corner of East 122nd Street is the rambling dwelling where Louise Boddie has lived for more than 60 years. The Boddie Recording Company sign tells you you've arrived at a singular place.

Tom Boddie, joined by his wife-to-be, operated the Boddie recording and pressing business out of 12202 Union Avenue beginning in 1959, when Leo's was still on Central Avenue and Gleason's Musical Bar on Woodland packed them in. Four years into their business partnership, Tom married the former Louise Stewart. In early years, the Boddie duo focused on recording, likely limited to one- and two-track affairs that would feature instrumentalists and vocalists together in the studio for a session. Such an arrangement made for tight quarters and the need for collaboration to make it all work. "One-take" recording also put pressure on all to be at their best; if the drummer missed his mark or a vocalist flubbed a lyric, then that recording was ruined—and expensive studio time and, perhaps, an otherwise-perfect take were wasted.

In 1968, the Boddies' business model broadened with the acquisition of their own record presses from some ambitious white boys. Boddie Recording was now more than just a service organization, selling recording time in the studio. Tom and Louise entered the manufacturing side of the business.

"Waxing" a record is complicated. At its core is a "biscuit," a "hockey-puck shaped piece of extruded vinyl between a label on the top and bottom," according to Gotta Groove Records, a Cleveland-based record-pressing company that owns an old Boddie record press. "The biscuit is compressed by the Record Press into the shape of a vinyl record."

For the next 25 years, the Boddie Recording Company was where groups hankering for fame or a memento could record 45s and 33s. The impact the Boddie operation had on Cleveland soul music, local artists, and local outlets can't be overestimated. Economic history shows that those mastering manufacturing and distribution enjoy greater control over their own destiny. The Boddies manufactured records, meaning steadier, more sustainable income for them and better chances for making artists' dreams come true.

A MARKET UNTO ITSELF

BEFORE BODDIE BECAME A FORCE it was an upstart, the first Black-owned recording studio in Cleveland. The embedded competition was provided by larger, established white-owned studios like Schneider Recording (where Tom apprenticed), Agency Recording and Cleveland Recording (the last occasionally sent masters to Boddie for pressing). Boddie was the go-to for a minority, predominantly Black, musical community, waxing acts like Lou Ragland's funky Hot Chocolate, groove masters Harvey and the Phenomenals, the apocalyptic Seven Revelators, the weird blues belter Delores White, and Los Nombres, a Latino band from Lorain.

The Boddies also recorded an O'Jays platter on contract for the Imperial label, laid down live in 1966 at Leo's Casino, and blues master Travis Haddix's debut 45 RPM single. That O'Jays album went unreleased, however, another notable but now invisible and unheard vestige of Cleveland's soul scene.

Boddie also recorded demos by white groups like Charade, a band that would later record a 45 for Epic. Buddy Maver, Charade's drummer and leader, recalls an afternoon when Charade recorded two songs at Boddie. The atmosphere was homey. "We had recorded at Cleveland Recording with Ken Hamann, and he was as white as Wonder Bread," Maver says.

"We could never get any big fat round bass sound or a good drum sound. We said, Let's give Boddie's a try; the price was right.

"We kind of thought, these are Black folks; let's see what kind of sound we could get. I think they recorded the bass and the drums better. At Boddie, we were able to take our time more."

WE COULD NEVER GET ANY BIG FAT ROUND BASS SOUND. WE SAID, LET'S GIVE BODDIE'S A TRY.

In the competitive recording world, being Black can be an advantage.

According to a May 1971 article in the long-defunct *Cleveland Press*, Tom bought his first disc recorder in 1941, before the advent of the tape recorder. As a youth, he experimented with recording in a coal shed at the rear of his family home on Kinsman Road near East 70th Street. He graduated from East Technical High School in 1942 with a major in industrial electricity. Shortly thereafter, he ran into racial discrimination when he was the only one in his otherwise all-white class to not land a job.

After military service during World War II, Tom returned to Cleveland, and in 1947 bought his first professional recorder. He made a living servicing radios, television sets and electronic organs (the great Hammond organist Eddie Baccus Sr. brought his B-3 to Boddie's for tuneups). Various Small Business Administration loans helped Tom and Louise buy the presses and a sealing machine. Another loan rebuilt the structure behind the house as a studio. According to the Press, Boddie "orders come from small groups, quartets, orchestras, traveling bands and singers who are able to sell their better recordings, or lease them to the big record companies."

Mrs. Boddie says her husband, who died of a brain aneurysm in 2006 at age 84, was the engineer and she was his "girl Friday. I did the bookkeeping, I did everything else. I could do everything. I could record. When it came to mixing it (a track) down, I could do that. I could do the whole function of the operation. We went out on site, I could do all of that…When he was here, he did it. But I could also do it."

Mrs. Boddie also learned to lay tile and pour cement so the couple could turn the former dairy barn behind their two-story home into a recording studio. Like so many other

Invisible Soul luminaries, thriving meant being willing to try anything, do anything in order to move ahead.

Boddie recordings were issued on labels such as Da-Wood, Day-Wood, Luau, Bounty and Wicked Lester. The Boddies didn't produce or sponsor artists, Mrs. Boddie says. "People would come in with their own material, but they didn't have a label, and some of them we put on our publishing company, Tomlou." In that case, the Boddies would buy the material, but they never had a hit so they never collected royalties. They recorded "every gospel group that lived in and around Cleveland, country and western from all over—West Virginia, primarily—soul music, jazz." They recorded Spanish groups, Caribbean groups, West Indian groups. Most Boddie recordings were in English; a few were in Spanish, which she understands. Mrs. Boddie's favorite music is country and western because "it's soothing. It's music you can travel by."

The Boddies' openness and eclecticism earned their operation the nickname "Little Nashville."

FROM SOUNDS TO SONGS

MRS. BODDIE SAYS THE couple secured a Small Business Administration loan for $15,000 in 1963. Ten years later, the SBA loaned them another $35,000. They used the latter to rebuild their crumbling garage. They tried for yet another loan, to build a small FM station, but, Mrs. Boddie says, bank officials didn't want Boddie to develop into another Motown, so they turned the application down.

I don't understand why a financial institution would turn down a thriving business' request for investment dollars to expand, but that's Mrs. Boddie's claim. A missing space on the Invisible Soul dial is a WBOD-FM station devoted to Boddie recordings that the Boddies might have launched.

Unlike Motown, Boddie never became a brand, let alone

An informal photo of Mrs. Boddie taken during my interview with her in 2011

a production company like Philadelphia International or Motown. It was a mom-and-pop, farm-to-table operation that never had the money to be that big.

Mrs. Boddie explains their mindset at that time. "I understand what happened with Motown is they sold shares… when you sell shares, at some point in time you got to reissue or stop, which we did not want. We wanted to own." (Motown was an independent company until founder Berry Gordy sold it for $61 million to MCA Records in 1988.)

"We struggled to stay here," she says. "We had the loans to pay back, we still had a lot of utilities, we had to run a new gas line from the street back to the garage, we had to run water lines back to the garage, and that was expensive because we had to have somebody come with the backhoe, then put in a new driveway—and it's 210 feet long."

But the Boddies did survive, paid back their loans, and worked long hours while keeping their rates affordable. The couple produced 12-inch 33s and seven-inch 45s in about equal numbers. In the later years of the Boddies' operation, the seven-inch singles dominated sales. Groups could record with less up-front investment, and the 45s were easier to carry to performances where groups sold them after the show. The Boddies charged customers about $500 to record and press 300 45s.

"We did more recording than we did pressing, but I guess our peak years were 1976 and 1977 because we were doing a lot of small jobs," she says. After that, business fell off when the oil crisis led to a shortage of shellac. In 1983, the pressing plant essentially shut down, she said, though the Boddies continued to record on the road.

In addition to operating their Union Avenue operation, they traveled to record speakers at conventions and other public engagements. They recorded sermons at exclusively Black churches and educational sessions at medical conferences. At the latter, Tom Boddie would set up portable recorders in multiple sessions, turning out cassettes on the spot. He was ahead of his time, recording and producing in real time, remotely. Still, those labor- and time-intensive sessions paled in comparison to the money and reputation the Boddies earned from their home operation.

THE PRESSES

THE WAY THE BODDIES acquired their presses is a story unto itself, a story now come full circle. According to journalist Laura Putre, writing in the online magazine The Root, they acquired the equipment from a Cleveland company called Kelmar in the late '60s. They had been using Kelmar to press their masters into records. Putre continued, in her October 13, 2010 article:

> "I would go over there, and they were teaching me how to operate the manual press," recalled Louise. Then the company lost some key investors and decided to close. "They said, 'would you all like to buy the equipment? We'll let you have it for a couple thousand dollars. ' "

"The Boddies managed to rustle up $2,100 to pay for two behemoth machines with manual presses. It took four minutes to press a record by hand. Louise did the manual labor, placing a ball of melted vinyl pellets into a lathe, then yanking down the heavy cover on the press. Each record took four minutes to set in the press, during which time Louise trimmed other records and put

A mundane county real estate photo can't capture the professional dynamic of the Boddie enterprise housed in the buildings on the left and rear.
(Photo courtesy of Cleveland Public Library)

them in sleeves."

The story varies by source. Here's Mrs. Boddie's version: The owners of Kelmar were the brothers Don and Tom King. Their presses were manual, and the Kings, who were white, didn't know how to run them, she said.

The Kings had pressed some records at Boddie, apparently because their own presses were manual. They asked Tom Boddie if he could automate their presses. He said he could convert them to semi-automatic. In addition, because Mrs. Boddie was quick with her hands pushing the biscuit of compressed vinyl pellets into the press and applying labels top and bottom, they wanted to hire her. But she said no.

Because the Kings didn't have the money to pay Tom Boddie for the work on the presses, they offered the Boddies stock as payment. Tom said OK, figuring if he and Louise owned stock in Kelmar, they'd have priority in pressing records. But when the Kings reported back to their "people" about that proposal, "what they did have a problem with was we would be part of the board," Mrs. Boddie says.

The King brothers owned 51 percent of Kelmar and voted the Boddies onto the board. At that point, the rest of the board quit. Without such support, the brothers had to sell, which is how and why the Boddies got Kelmar's presses, she says. "We probably would not have been going to any of the board meetings anyway. We were too busy trying to get our own thing together out here. We were an asset, not a liability, to them. That was so crazy. That was the dumbest thing they could have done."

Tom King, who died on April 23, 2011, led a band called

the Starfires and co-wrote the pop-rock classic "Time Won't Let Me" for the Outsiders. His brother, Don, called Mrs. Boddie's account "misinformation."

In a telephone interview from his home in Lakewood, Don King (not the boxing promoter) said he was chief engineer at Kelmar Records and the Boddies had nothing to do with construction of the facility. King said Tom Boddie "knew nothing about pressing records," and King electroplated the masters, made stampers and operated the extruder. He said he, not Tom Boddie, was automating the presses.

He quit Kelmar when investors pulled out, effectively ending the company. He also seemed contradictory about Tom Boddie, calling him incompetent in one breath and praising him in the next. King said Tom Boddie was "a very talented man, a brilliant man," adding he would gladly have helped the Boddies with their operation but "I was never asked."

Too bad the two companies couldn't get along.

Fast-forward to 2011, when Gotta Groove Records, the only record pressing plant in Cleveland, bought one of the original Kelmar Fine-Bilt presses and a vinyl extruder from Mrs. Boddie, moving it to Gotta Groove's downtown plant that September. (The only other plant in Ohio is Musicol Recording in Columbus, recording since 1966 and pressing vinyl since 1971.)

Vince Slusarz, Gotta Groove's founder and owner, said the "press is a semi-automatic, you can do a 12-inch record, you can do a seven-inch record."

That wooden sign on Union and the sale to Gotta Groove weren't the only signs of life sparked courtesy of the Boddie legacy. In November 2011, Numero Group, a "soul archeologist" label from Chicago, released Boddie Recording Company: Cleveland, Ohio, a three-CD set featuring 58 tracks culled from hundreds the Boddies laid down in their sprawling complex. Boddie continues to resonate.

The 3-CD Boddie set has sold about 7,000 copies, a testament to the Boddie legacy.

The Boddie enterprise lives deep in the collective memory of artists who recorded there, people who worked there, and fans who bought records waxed there. And, while the family business is long gone, Mrs. Boddie still lives in that big house, and the distinctive Boddie logo remains a fixture on Union Avenue. Some might see that sign and the Boddie property as nagging reminders of what might have been even more spectacular. Some might see it as something even more enduring in a positive way.

It seems that good things come to those who wait.

In late summer 2023, Cleveland City Council made the Boddie complex a Cleveland Landmark.

Louise Boddie addressed that decisive August 18 meeting, saying she was honored to see all the support for the designation. Dennis Boddie noted that his parents, Tom and Louise, made location recordings at Leo's Casino for Jackie Wilson, Aretha Franklin and the Temptations.

"He recorded any and everybody," Dennis said of his father. "It was for giving people the opportunity of being a star in music."

Cleveland City Councilman Kevin Conwell recalled recording at Boddie in 1978, and said the studio's history needs to be recognized, according to ideastream Public Media/wosu.org.

"When you look at the Rock and Roll Hall of Fame, it's not telling the story," said Conwell, who is also a drummer. "So we must go beyond this legislation so our children know the background history."

"There's a saying in preservation that the history of a place is not always obvious," City Planner Karl Brunjes said. "Architectural significance can be identified by sight. Cultural significance, on the other hand, often hides in plain sight."

What is clear to me is that any successful preservation of assets like Boddie is far better than the brutal evisceration of inner city East Side properties over the past 60 years.

A second, better-known pillar of Cleveland's soul scene today has zero physical presence or artifacts viewable on the street. But when this soul sanctuary was hot, Cleveland basked in its glow.

And it glowed red hot.

LEO'S
Sets the Stage

LEO FRANK'S AND JULES BERGER'S CLUB WAS built and operated to be cozy and expansive at the same time. For the audience, Leo's felt like home. For management and talent, the club was large enough to persuade even the hottest national acts to add it to their tour list.

Like good house parties that always seem to wind up in the kitchen, Leo's main showroom, located in the basement, was an improbable location for a concert venue. More than 700 music lovers could be accommodated, ensuring both a rewarding take from ticket sales and profitability. Thirsty patrons were served at bars front and back, and shows were presented Thursday through Sunday nights, along with a Sunday matinee most weeks.

Among the performers who graced Leo's stage: major and lesser Motown acts, along with Aretha Franklin, Dionne Warwick, Otis Redding, B.B. King (once, in a monster 10-day run in 1965), jazz trumpeter Dizzy Gillespie, saxophonist Julian "Cannonball" Adderley and organist "Brother" Jack McDuff, singer Nina Simone, and comedians Redd Foxx, a novice Flip Wilson, Dick Gregory, and Richard Pryor. Gregory called Leo's the most integrated club in America.

Those who frequented Leo's Casino in the former Quad Hall Hotel at 7500 Euclid Avenue are wistful about this entertainment mecca and miss the community it symbolized.

It was a place to see, and a place where one vied to be seen. It was above all a haven for music aficionados.

Search "live Cleveland soul music" and hundreds of entries pop up. Most of those links lead to a long-gone basement club on Euclid Avenue. Leo's Casino was the cornerstone of all that was special about Cleveland's soul scene. While the Boddie legacy retains a physical presence, no vestige of Leo's remains. But make no mistake — Leo's was real, special and worthy of celebrating and preserving.

Leo's "was big enough to hold anybody that was big in those days that had a record out," says vocalist, producer and arranger Bobby Massey. "It was the top club in Cleveland. Everything was good.

"When they didn't have a show, they didn't open the back room—but you could always go there and have a drink," recalls Massey, a founding member of the O'Jays and the group's business manager until 1972, when it signed with the Philadelphia International label. The O'Jays began as an opening act at Leo's, sharing the limelight with such other local talents as the Sahibs and the Wigs. The O'Jays eventually became massively popular, moving up the soul success ladder from opening act to headliner and eventually, in 1972, a breakout national phenomenon with the paranoid, urgent "Back Stabbers."

It was more than just the songs' messages that made the O'Jays so infectious. It was also the passion, the synchronized and sensual moves, and above all, Eddie Levert's high, gritty tenor. His voice was so expressive it simultaneously incorporated supplication and assertion, no mean feat. Thom Bell's widescreen arrangements set the group in high relief, too. Although they started as a quintet in their native Canton, their most durable component was the trio of Levert, Walter Williams, and William Powell. They moved as one, three voices slipping in and out of each other.

Besides their musical talent and sense of showmanship, the success of the group can also be attributed to being well-connected early on.

"Leo Frank and Jules Berger were the O'Jays managers so we worked with Dionne Warwick and Flip Wilson whenever they got in," Massey told the *Plain Dealer* in 2017. "The club had a small intimate atmosphere. Every seat was a good seat and there was good sound and a stage that you could look out and see everybody and everybody could see you. It was one of the top clubs in the country. They booked anybody that was anybody. It was one of the first clubs where blacks and whites came together and attracted people from the West Side."

"Leo's Casino is where Motown came to find out if they were up to snuff," says the Cleveland vocalist Art Blakey.

"Remember, this is when everybody was fresh. You had people like Chuck Jackson, Bobby 'Blue' Bland, everybody came there. B.B. King, Temptations, Smokey and the Miracles, Martha and the Vandellas, Supremes, Marvin Gaye, the Spinners.

"The Hough Riots were going on," Blakey says. "Leo's was on Euclid, the riots were two streets over. Yet white people from the suburbs and the West Side would pack Leo's

WHAT WAS SO SPECIAL ABOUT LEO'S? THE MUSIC, YEAH. BUT YOU'D LOOK AROUND, AND EVERYONE WAS SMILING.

Casino during that time. That shows you how the music drew the people anyway."

LEI LADY LEI

"THE ONLY CLUB I hung out in was Leo's Casino on Sunday afternoon," says Charm Warren-Celestine, the stepdaughter of Wilbur Dean, the man behind Dean's House of Jazz.

"Back in the day, the Temptations or the O'Jays would come to Leo's for three or four nights; the Temptations and the O'Jays were just as popular to people under 18 as over 18," says Warren-Celestine, who grew up in the music business.

There were battles of the bands, what the jazzerati call "cutting contests."

"The O'Jays were local heroes, and because of that Detroit-Cleveland competitiveness—some people say the 'mistake on the lake' is Cleveland but some say it's Detroit—they would do rounds. And every Sunday afternoon when the performers' demographic was under 18, they would have a matinee at Leo's."

Warren-Celestine started going there in her early teens. "It was a safe place," she says. "My Dad knew the guy at the door, they weren't serving liquor, it was a group of us, and he had to come back to pick us up. We didn't leave that building until he picked us up."

If Leo's was integral to Cleveland's music scene 60 and 70 years ago, so was *Upbeat*, Herman Spero's Saturday-afternoon show on WEWS Channel 5. "I went to Leo's every Thursday night because everybody who was on Leo's was on *Upbeat*," says Herman's son David, a music-industry lifer who entered that business through his father's show. *Upbeat* showcased local, regional and national bands.

On December 9, 1967, the great soul singer Otis Redding appeared on *Upbeat* and then performed at Leo's on the second night of a two-night stand. The next day, he and four-fifths of the Bar-Kays, his backup band, died in a plane crash in Madison, Wisconsin.

In a weird coincidence, Redding's final performance, at Leo's, took place the same night Cleveland trumpeter Kenny Davis journeyed to Central State College in Wilberforce, Ohio as a member of the O'Jays band. "Another band opened for us," Davis recalled. "As it turned out, we should have opened for them.

"Here we are in tuxedos, and here these guys are. One's got a diaper on with a great big safety pin, and one's in overalls. Police are holding everybody back while these guys are smoking herb right there in the other room." That opener—like the O'Jays, this group would soon headline—was Parliament-Funkadelic, George Clinton's surreal funk band. Soul music knows no boundaries.

"When we got back from that gig, Otis Redding was coming out of Leo's," Davis says. "We talked to Otis when they were packing."

Leo's, meanwhile, felt safe and accessible, according to David Spero, who with his brother Harry went there Thursday nights with their father. Herman Spero brought the boys along as he kibitzed with groups scheduled to appear on *Upbeat* on Saturday. "It was a combination of business and pleasure," Spero recalls. "We always had to wear sports jackets and ties. The tables were very close, and it was incredibly smoky.

"No matter where you were, you weren't far from the stage. Wayne Cochran and the C.C Riders, that (group) was probably 12, 14 people; the Temptations had a pretty good-size band behind them. So the stage was probably pretty deep."

Very few white bands played Leo's, Spero says, but "on the weekend of the Hough Riots, wouldn't you know it was Wayne Cochran and the C.C. Riders headlining the club."

"Blue eyed soul brother" Cochran was known for his platinum-colored, architectural hairdo and over-the-top shows. Known as the white James Brown, Cochran left soul music to become a preacher.

Leo's was hospitable, but there were rules. "We checked IDs every day, every show," says Freddie Arrington, who in 1957 began working for Leo Frank at the latter's original club and was emcee at Leo's Casino into the late '60s. "And if you were under age—people had to have an ID—we'd let them in. But they'd have to wear a lei around their neck. That way waitresses knew, and if there was any question about anybody, they'd call me."

EARLY DAYS

THE LEO'S ERA BEGAN in 1952 when Navy veteran Frank opened his first club at East 49th Street and Central Avenue. The building was near competitor William "Jap" Gleason's Musical Bar at East 55th Street and Woodland Avenue. At the time, jazz was truly popular; doo-wop, which showcased harmony vocals, was on the rise, but rhythm and blues, let alone soul, was not yet on the horizon.

Frank launched his venture at 4805-17 Central as a neighborhood tavern, sharing a wall with Abbott's Bar-B-Q. The one-story building was situated triangularly on the northeast corner. It presented jazz by the likes of Jimmy Smith and Cannonball Adderley, as well as Aretha Franklin in her teen years. Whites dotted the neighborhood.

In November 1958, the *Call & Post* celebrated entrepreneurs Frank and Abbott for a remodeling that gave "this combination of enterprises an edifice of breathtaking beauty." As further inducement, the two men announced that "all highballs and cocktails are offered at greatly reduced prices during the lengthy luncheon period, 11:30 a.m. until 5 p.m. daily." Air-conditioning was another draw. No wonder those business lunches lasted and lasted and lasted.

The original Leo's, along with John Abbott's eatery, burned to the ground on Christmas Eve 1962, displacing 20 residents of tenements above and to the rear of the businesses. According to the *Call & Post*, the blaze, of unknown origin, wreaked $75,000 in damages—nearly a quarter of a million dollars in 2023 money.

On September 16, 1963, Frank and his new business partner Jules Berger launched Leo's Casino at 7500 Euclid; the first act in the new digs was vocalist Gloria Lynne. While the club drew fans of all complexions, the neighborhood was predominantly Black.

Buddy Maver, a white drummer who led several rock bands and also managed the Agora, spoke fondly of Leo's.

"Before the Hough Riots, there were black-and-tan clubs where everybody went to groove to the music and nobody bothered anybody," he recalls. "I think Black people knew if they saw some white people, the white people were there because they loved the music. Leo's was the preeminent black-and-tan club. People used to get dressed up to the nines to go to Leo's."

White fans, says Maver, spiffed up, too—in a sincere form of flattery. Here is how he described the scene:

> Back in those days, we used to buy all our clothes at Jerry Mills and Harry Weintraub's on Prospect Avenue between 9th Street and 4th Street. They had all the clothes the Black guys were wearing: shirts with the high-boy collars, pants with the dropped loops so you had your shirt tucked in and there was this much material above a little skinny white belt; you always had to wear the buckle on the side. And on Euclid Avenue, between 9th Street and Public Square, there were literally about 15 men's shoe stores: Flagg Bros., Florsheim, John Hardy. You had to buy real pointy black shoes with white stitching and had to be careful when you shined them. When the Beatles came out, everything changed.

"White people used to line up at Leo's to see the Motown groups," says Eddie Brown, a Black guitarist who briefly performed with the Imperial Wonders, Cleveland's

answer to the Temptations. "It was a very cosmopolitan-type atmosphere." Was there racial tension? "None whatsoever, because everybody was about music. It wasn't a prejudiced club at all because Leo Frank and Jules Berger owned Leo's Casino.

"The Home of the Stars, that's what they called it."

A COMPLEX ENTERPRISE

FREDDIE ARRINGTON SIGNED ONTO Leo's early. He calls himself a "bottom-line adviser" to Leo Frank, emceeing shows at Leo's Casino during most of the '60s. He also hired local talent to spice up the shows, like comedians Charles Eckstein and Eli Tel a Lie, a Detroit character whose motto was "Eli Tel a Lie, Faster Than You Can Bat an Eye." Arrington ultimately hired Tel a Lie to run the lights and sound system at Leo's, a steady job that paid better than stand-up.

When Frank and Berger reopened Leo's, on Euclid, in the fall of 1963, they were able to leverage their success at presenting jazz into the growing world of soul. Expanding from a venue with a capacity of about 300 to one of more than 700 helped. So did the club's reputation for integration in a racially charged period. That decade, Arrington combined his work at Leo's with being a salesman for Seagram's. Hustle always matters.

IN THE LINE OF FIRE

NOT ALL WAS KUMBAYA in those volatile days, however, and Cleveland wasn't exactly peaceful. Nearly two years before the Hough Riots tore the city apart, the singer Gloria Lynne was shot in the upper left leg as "she stepped up on the bandstand of Leo's Casino in downtown Cleveland to the cheers of the fans she had attracted to the nightclub," said *The Afro American.*

"Suddenly, the place was buzzing with bullets," the newspaper reported in October 1964. "A wild gun duel had developed outside between police and an unidentified Indian youth who had tried to stick up a nearby tavern, and stray bullets whizzed through the doors and windows of the nightclub." People ducked under tables. Lynne was sent to the hospital and eventually convalesced in her New York apartment.

The *Call & Post* was more informative. The weekly said the singer was "skinned" on the right thigh "with a stray pellet from a shotgun blast" that killed the suspect in the attempted robbery. Lynne had just finished "an appearance on stage and was walking through the kitchen to get to the lounge."

Lynne's accidental wounding was an exception, however. Leo's Casino was above all a musical magnet, and a place where an artist could develop—fast. It was a great hang, too.

Don George, a "record guy" who worked in promotion for numerous labels, went to Leo's every Thursday night, opening night for the big acts. George, who died in early 2021, remembered playing pool there with Jerry "the Iceman" Butler, the original lead singer of the Impressions—and, George said, still smarting—Butler won big. George went to shows at Leo's for years, and vividly recalls one night starring George Clinton, ringleader of Parliament-Funkadelic, that stoned-out band Kenny Davis encountered in concert in Wilberforce.

Photographer George Shuba captures O'Jays wardrobe valet Andrew Levert outside Leo's in 1967.

George said Clinton threw down a territorial challenge, saying "something to the effect that, I hear this is O'Jays country. Clinton said, Move over, we're going to kick ass; they had many hits after that. That was Funkadelic."

George also caught two nights of Dionne Warwick at Leo's in what might have been her debut gig. "She was just so nervous; it wasn't a great show the first night," George says. "I went back Sunday night and she was phenomenal."

Halfway through her Sunday night performance, Warwick apologized for her debut, and thanked Jules Berger for inviting her to a cookout and making her feel more comfortable. "She said, I really appreciate the way you appreciated me tonight. She was almost in tears."

LOCAL BOYS

THE BIG MOTOWN ACTS brought their own rhythm sections to Leo's, but it was up to the locals to supply the horns. One of the key Clevelanders was Davis, the trumpet player who kept crossing paths with Parliament-Funkadelic.

Davis became a professional in the early '60s following a stint in the U.S. Navy Band. He worked all over 105 in its heyday, starting with a steady gig in the house band at the Circle Ballroom on Euclid at 105th. He rubbed shoulders with legends.

Davis recalls a time in the early '60s when a musician from Detroit dropped in with the blueprint of a song. "A guy comes in with the lead sheet, sits down at this piano and plays this tune. He didn't have any music, but we had listened to his records so we knew what they sounded like," Davis says. "It was Marvin Gaye. That was the beginning of that, when the Motown circuit started to come to Cleveland."

Davis played jazz, soul, pop, whatever the gig demanded. For a time, he was a member of the Futuretones, a doo-wop group that evolved into Cleveland's first full band. According to Maggie Evans, the widow of guitarist Russell Evans, the Futuretones backed up visiting musicians such as Warwick, Gaye, and other Motown acts at Leo's. Russell Evans worked in the Futuretones and later in the O'Jays.

Eventually, Davis became a member of a de facto house band at Leo's, which at one time or another included trumpeter-turned-bassist Tom Baker, trombonist Fred Wheatt, saxophonists Augustus Hawkins, Ernie Krivda, Willie Smith, and Don Kubec, drummer Val Kent, and guitarist Lou Ragland. Hawkins died of Covid-19 in October 2020. Ragland, a musical giant who played many roles in Cleveland's music industry, died of cancer in August 2020.

LEO'S CASINO IN CONTEXT

TOM BAKER, A CLEVELAND native versed in virtually all musical styles, worked in two widely disparate house bands: at Leo's Casino and at Roger Bohn's Smiling Dog Saloon on West 25th Street. The Smiling Dog lasted from 1971 to 1975. Between those two clubs, music fans could absorb the most modern and sophisticated sounds of the day during a period of singular musical ferment and creativity.

"Leo's Casino was strictly the pop scene, mainly Motown and O'Jays," says Baker, who crafted arrangements for the O'Jays early on. "I would say Black pop; Motown was not really r&b. It was Black pop music.

"The Smiling Dog Saloon was primarily a jazz venue with some pop artists, and the performers were from all walks: Black, white, Hispanic, and with a huge, completely mixed audience. Leo's Casino was very small and Smiling Dog was very large. If a Motown act was performing at Leo's, the place would be standing room only. At the Smiling Dog, if it was a well-known, primary artist, it would be packed; if it wasn't so well known it would probably be half-full." Leo's was basically a "storefront type venue," Smiling Dog a standalone building. Baker worked for Frank and Berger from 1965 to 1969.

IF A MOTOWN ACT WAS PERFORMING AT LEO'S, THE PLACE WOULD BE STANDING ROOM ONLY.

Another notable, if short-lived, club was the Jazz Temple at Mayfield Road and Euclid, on the current site of the Museum of Contemporary Art Cleveland. Launched by 105-area entrepreneur Winston Willis and his girlfriend, Charlene Hurd, it featured major jazz figures but, due to bombings and other threats likely linked to its proximity to the famously racist Little Italy neighborhood, it shut down for good in 1963.

Baker saw the volcanic jazz saxophonist John Coltrane at the Jazz Temple.

"I can see that clear as day in my mind's eye right now, sitting in the audience, no one on stage, and the door next to the stage open to the audience," he recalled. The group walked on stage, took their coats off, and set up. Then they counted off the first tune. "It was completely unlike Leo's—do an intro and introduce the act. Talk about earthy, man. The set-up was this crude thing and the John Coltrane Quartet was the best. They went through walking through the door, to all of a sudden counting off and they're going, man." (Coltrane played Leo's July 24-29, 1962.)

Kenny Davis, that trumpeter about town, speaks of a show of similar impact—at Leo's.

"One day we were at Leo's in the house band, and Leo and Jules said, 'Look, we got a band coming in this week that's self-contained so we don't need your horns but you can come to the show for free,'" he recalls. "It was Sly and the Family Stone. We went there, saw them; I wasn't the same since. It was just wonderful, man. Come on—'Stand,' 'Thank You (Falettinme Be Mice Elf Agin)'".

Working at Leo's "was fun because we didn't realize it was history, we just knew it was a gig. We'd come in, they'd say we got so-and-so coming in this week, we got rehearsal, we'd hit the same night. We worked Thursday through Sunday, one show on Thursday and

Friday and Saturday, maybe two on Sunday." Good pay? "For then? Shit, it was money."

FADING OUT

THE SUPREMES WERE SO hot in the summer of 1966 that their album, *The Supremes A' Go-Go*, bumped the Beatles' *Revolver* off the top of the charts. Here's a glimpse of their activity in Cleveland that July. It comes from a quirky website called concerts.fandom.com:

Leo Frank, activist Ruth Turner, comedian Dick Gregory and Leo's Casino revered frontman Freddie Arrington (Cleveland Public Library)

> July 14-19, 1966 Leo's Casino, Cleveland, OH, two shows each night. This engagement was disturbed by the Hough Riots that began just a few blocks away between 8 and 9 p.m. on July 18 (and ended on July 23-24). The mayor ordered all the bars and cafes in the Hough neighborhood closed on July 19. Most probably the second concert of July 18 was canceled, as were those of July 19.

According to a 2017 *Plain Dealer* article, the Supremes also "rode into town to play three shows at the club July 24—in a Cadillac they had borrowed from Motown mogul Berry Gordy." Supreme Mary Wilson said the group didn't know what to expect. They performed two of the shows; the National Guard ordered the third canceled to restore calm.

"America might have been segregated, but there were these iconic places like Leo's where people came together," says Wilson, whose earliest shows outside of Detroit took place in Cleveland. "Leo's was part of that golden moment in time where music showed Americans what we had in common."

But economics began to take its toll on Leo's as performers who were a bargain to book at the onset of their careers demanded and commanded higher prices as their popularity swelled. Musical tastes changed. Cleveland's population hemorrhaged and aftershocks from the Hough Riots and the Glenville Shootout almost exactly two years later didn't help the club, either.

Berger and Frank grew increasingly disaffected and shut down Leo's in 1972. Frank died in July 1999. His Associated Press obituary identified him as "a nightclub owner honored two weeks ago by Dionne Warwick for boosting the early careers of performers including herself, Aretha Franklin, and Stevie Wonder." Warwick and Frank appeared together that June "at a ceremony dedicating a plaque designating the former Leo's site as a landmark in the development of rock music."

Most memories fade fast. Memories of Leo's fade slowly. We should be thankful that some of those memories remain.

SHARE YOUR LEO'S EXPERIENCE - stories, memories, photos.
Connect with us at invisiblesoul.act3creative.com
or text 216.373.7676

Scan to upload photos, then click the blue "Send a File?" button

6 MOTOWN'S *Fateful Shadow*

The crosscurrents between Cleveland and Detroit could run fast and fruitful. But those ties could also bind, discourage, and damage relationships, performers, and souls.

O THIS DAY, MANY CONSIDER MOTOWN soul's premier brand. Musicianship, a diversity of stars, and cultural influence are its hallmarks. Like Detroit automobiles, hits from Berry Gordy's family of labels drilled deep into white households in the '60s, contributing to the soundtrack for civil rights and, at the end of the decade, the antiwar movement. Less earthy than Stax-Volt or Atlantic, other record labels famous for soul music, Motown delivered a sound that was long on treble and perfect for AM radio. No wonder Gordy pushed it so successfully as the "Sound of Young America."

Despite rolling memorable tunes out of Detroit like an assembly line, and the high profile of such acts as Smokey Robinson and the Miracles, the Four Tops, the Supremes with and without Diana Ross, the Temptations, Marvin Gaye and Stevie Wonder, Motown cast a pall over some of its own, stars and sidemen alike. While some Motown artists became celebrities, others, including the key sidemen known as the Funk Brothers, were kept in the background, underpaid, under-credited and, in some cases, outright neglected.

Time to shine a light on Cleveland musicians connected, however tenuously, to Motown, because Motown cast its shadow well beyond Detroit. It loomed over Cleveland from the early '60s through the '70s, when promising groups from the northern Ohio city had a chance for a Motown audition, had a family tie to the Gordy clan, or, in some cases, even recorded for a Detroit label Gordy's empire had absorbed.

A MIXED PICTURE

CLEVELAND SOUL MUSICIANS RARELY made a lasting mark by way of Motown, and even when they did, the picture was murky. Success followed by disappointment, overreach and insufficient diligence mark the fitful relationship between the Detroit powerhouse and the Cleveland soul scene. This is a chapter about almost making it.

One of the strongest links between the cities was Leo's Casino, which has been called "Cleveland's Motown outpost." Motown used Leo's to road-test its acts, and when Motown bands headlined, Cleveland's finest opened. Leo's was a must stop on the Chitlin' Circuit back in the day.

Despite their exposure at Leo's, few of the local acts that performed there made it onto a Motown label. The O'Jays were the best-known Cleveland-based performers at Leo's, but they ended up on Kenny Gamble and Leon Huff's Philadelphia International, a stiff competitor to Motown in the '70s. The Dazz Band did make it onto the actual Motown label, and did very well—for a time. The same went for Charles Hatcher after he evolved into Edwin Starr.

Tom Baker was responsible for adding Cleveland horns to the rhythm sections Motown acts brought to Leo's from Detroit. A gifted arranger whose string voicings mark numerous Cleveland pop and soul records, Baker explored a deal with Motown but ultimately walked away.

Encouraged by a producer at Motown whom he had impressed, Baker ventured to Detroit at the end of the '60s with his attorney, ready to talk terms. It is hard to pin down dates. Even the participants, who certainly have long—if fading—memories, are short on detail.

Baker says he progressed far enough with Motown to start a conversation about contract obligations. He listened as his advocate explored details with a Motown lawyer, but "at one point my attorney said, 'This is a slavery contract.'" The conversation ended there.

Others, like Bill Jacocks and Willie Smith, forged a professional relationship with Motown.

Jacocks, a Tennessee native and self-taught musician who grew up in Cleveland, may be known best for becoming the first regularly scheduled Black television anchorman in Cleveland, in 1975 on WEWS/Channel 5. From 1963 to 1964, Jacocks wrote songs for Motown's main publishing arm, Jobete Music, working out of Jobete's Brill Building office in New York City. None of Jacocks's Jobete tunes became hits.

Smith had a higher Motown profile. The Cleveland native worked for the house that Gordy built for seven years in the '60s. Smith told Cleveland jazz historian Joe Mosbrook he escorted and wrote for Stevie Wonder, Diana Ross, the Tops, the Temptations, Martha and the Vandellas, Smokey Robinson, and Marvin Gaye: "We would take them out and I was writing for them," Smith told Mosbrook. At home in both soul and jazz, Smith contributed orchestrations and a tune to 52nd Street Themes, a Blue Note album Cleveland jazz saxophone giant Joe Lovano released in 2000. Smith died of colon cancer in 2009.

Another Cleveland band to have a brush with Motown fame was Sly, Slick & Wicked. After recording a single for James Brown's short-lived People label, John F. Wilson (Sly), Charles Still (the main Slick) and various Wickeds recorded for local labels and some national labels, including a Motown subsidiary.

Jacocks, Smith and Sly, Slick & Wicked are largely inside stories. The Dazz Band and Edwin Starr developed high public profiles on Gordy-related labels—respectively Motown and Tamla. And in both cases, Motown's support waned, effectively stranding those artists.

That's also what happened to Ann Bogan, a singer who grew up in Cleveland's Fairfax neighborhood. She began vocalizing in Emmanuel Baptist Church and in her teens joined The Challengers III, a Cleveland group that recorded in Detroit for Tri-Phi, a label owned by Harvey Fuqua of the Moonglows (an influential doo-wop group featuring a precocious Marvin Gaye) and an early architect of Motown. Fuqua's Moonglows left quite a mark.

A special type of vocal was a Moonglows trademark according to Harvey Hall, who patterned his Fabulous Five Flames after Fuqua's foundational group.

"It was called 'blow' harmony," Hall said. "It was a vocal style in which you used air to emphasize notes. Instead of doing straight chords—it was chords, but instead of singing 'whoo,' like that, it was like, 'Whoo': They would blow it out. It became a style for them. Nobody else did it. It was just a bunch of guys messin' around."

Bogan, meanwhile, had her own harmonic style, singing with George Hendricks in the Challengers. She said "Honey Honey Honey," a tune the group wrote and the Challengers' first single, was a No. 1 hit in 1962 on WJMO, the AM station Ken Hawkins headed. Bogan said she alone wrote the B-side, "Stay With Me." In any case, the connection between Bogan and Fuqua was made—and was, apparently, solid.

"Honey Honey Honey" is a yearning tune with insistent piano, ringing guitar, and Bogan's persuasive, churchy lead. It's become a Northern Soul favorite. But subsequent

Challengers III 45s failed to sell, and a follow-up group called the Executives fizzled; so did a 1962 recording Bogan and Fuqua made for Fuqua's Harvey label.

Bogan also briefly sang with the Andantes, Motown's house vocalists (in effect the Funk Sisters), and replaced Marvelettes founder Gladys Horton in time to sing on the 1969 album *In Full Bloom*. Hers is largely a tale of missed opportunities.

Bogan had her moment in the Motown sun, but a growing family prompted her to quit the Marvelettes in 1970. She resurfaced in Love, Peace & Happiness and, eventually, New Birth, groups Fuqua managed that recorded for RCA. Sporting African dress and a dynamic Afro, Bogan looks beautiful on cover pictures of Love, Peace & Happiness and New Birth LPs. Bogan also said she was called to audition for the Supremes in 1964 but couldn't go because she was pregnant; Cindy Birdsong got the spot instead. Meanwhile, in 1967, she was tapped for the Marvelettes slot and stayed with the group for five or six years. Bogan sings on the Marvelettes' *Sophisticated Soul* album.

Bogan said she made money from Motown only by performing, but never earned any royalties. Kinship, exemplified by Marvelette Wanda Young's marriage to Bobby Rogers of the Miracles, helped at Motown.

"I think I could sing just as good as Diana (Ross), Mary Wells, all of them," she said. "But I wasn't in that little family group. I enjoyed what little I did do; I got the chance to go places I know I never would have."

Fuqua, who died in 2011, was married to Berry Gordy's baby sister Gwen. By 1965, he headed Motown's Artists Development Department. Too few of his Cleveland connections amounted to much.

"The musicians were nice," Bogan said, "but like I say, it's things I don't even want to say… I'll just say everybody wasn't treated the same."

At least Bogan recorded for Motown and other major labels and, while her story has its share of regret, others are grimmer. Take these accounts from members of the Sahibs, True Movement—and the Sensations, a short-lived vocal group that might have gotten in on the ground floor of Gordy's empire had they dreamed big enough to make the move.

ALL MISS, NO HIT

THAT ELUSIVE DOO-WOP GROUP the Sahibs drove to Detroit at the dawn of the '60s to see whether they could hook up with Motown. They didn't just fail; they were humiliated, despite the indisputable talents of all-around entertainer George Hendricks, the captivating vocalist Art Blakey and the multi-talented Lou Ragland.

Hendricks said the Sahibs played in a union hall, but further details are lacking. WJMO's Ken Hawkins arranged the tryout. The wintertime date also featured the Contours, Mary Wells, and Popcorn and the Mohawks; Richard Wylie's instrumental group backed all the acts—except the Sahibs, the only one from out of town.

Because the people who ran the show wouldn't let Popcorn and the Mohawks back them, the Cleveland group had to rely solely on a guitarist. Hendricks noted the Sahibs were basically a cappella and not used to working with a band.

Despite a warm reception for their two songs, the situation deteriorated: The Sahibs returned to their dressing rooms only to discover that they'd been ripped off, and that all they owned was the shirts on their backs.

"There was a nice response from the crowd," Hendricks said. "It was just that when we went back to the dressing room, our clothes were gone. The killer part was there was a guy who was supposed to be watching. He was gone, too."

Hendricks' uncle, who lived in Detroit, quickly arranged a gig at a bowling alley so the group could raise enough gas money to stuff themselves, a guitar and amplifier into a Pontiac for the drive back to Cleveland.

BALL OF CONFUSION

IN 1974, ANOTHER CLEVELAND group tried to hook up with the Motown operation. True Movement consisted of tenors Ernest Mims, John Cofer and Kenny Redd. Phil

Coghill provided bottom as bass-baritone. Their manager, Leonard Jackson, told Coghill Motown "was looking for another group to come behind the Temptations."

Motown had sent two songwriters to Miystic (cq) Insight, True Movement's label, to scout out the act. According to Coghill, Jackson sent the Motown, Sony and Atlantic record labels copies of True Movement's 45, "What a Lovely Way To Meet/Depression." It seemed True Movement was a contender.

Then things got complicated. Call it inside-label conflict.

Besides True Movement, Jackson managed Lou Ragland's Hot Chocolate, along with the singer Sonny Lovell, who like True Movement recorded for Miystic Insight.

Jackson insisted Motown sign a package deal for all the Miyistic Insight artists. Motown said no. Meanwhile, Coghill and the other Movements jumped the gun, so sure they would be signed to Motown they had started to spread the news.

"We had going away parties—'Motown wants us, we're gone!'—We got on the radio, played the record, did an interview, everything," Coghill says.

"Then Motown pulled the deal," he says. "Jackson was trying to play hardball with the biggies, but they said, 'We don't need you, you need us.' By that time, the other companies had got off the table anyway because Motown had taken the lead. And they were offering the most money."

For a minute, True Movement looked to be on a fast track to the big time, but tough business dealings slammed the brakes on their dream. True Movement lost so much face it disbanded. You can sense his eyes rolling behind his shades as Coghill relives the story.

SO CLOSE ...

AT LEAST TRUE MOVEMENT got to the talking stage with Motown. The Sensations, a singing group that only existed for a year, never got that far. More than 50 years ago, Abdul Ghani was a member of the Sensations and its predecessor, the El Deons, a doo-wop group that headlined teen dances with such contemporaries as the Futuretones, the La Salles and Las Toreadors. He's sheepish when he talks about the interaction between the Sensations and that man about Motown, Harvey Fuqua.

(Don't confuse these Sensations with a Michigan band that recorded in the mid-'60s, a Philadelphia group that recorded in the mid-'50s, or the Motown cover band of that name, an all-white quintet that worked Cleveland clubs into this century. Ghani said his Sensations recorded two tunes but they were never released.)

Ghani is a short, compact man who became a Muslim nearly 60 years ago. Born Edward Lee Williams, he used to be a slim, sharply coiffed teenager who fluttered little girls' hearts so, an La Deonettes fan club formed.

One day in 1961, Ghani heard Fuqua on WABQ pushing the Spinners' first record, "That's What Girls Are Made For." So Ghani went to the daytime AM station and asked DJ Eddie O'Jay whether the Sensations could audition for Fuqua.

O'Jay said sure, directing the Sensations to the Crosstown Motel at East 55th Street and Central Avenue, across from the tony Majestic Hotel, the key gathering spot for Black entertainers. Fuqua wasn't there, so Ghani went to the Cleveland Arena to kill time watching friends box.

When he returned to the Crosstown, Ghani found Fuqua but not the other Sensations. So he got William Justice out of bed, rounded up William Burwell from someplace on 115th Street—and learned that Garfield "Buddy" Jackson was at the lake messing around with Burwell's sister.

After rousting Jackson, the group went back to the Crosstown and sang for Fuqua until 4 or 5 in the morning. Fuqua gave Ghani Anna Gordy's card and said, "You guys just get to Motown. You don't have to worry about anything. You just get to Motown."

The group never made it to Detroit. Ghani has regretted that for decades.

"We didn't know for sure if it was for real and we didn't have financial means to get there," Ghani says. "I had a little old car that might have gotten us there. Going to Detroit was like going to the moon.

"If we had gone to Motown, we would have been in that first family of Motown, we would have been with the Temptations, the Miracles, the Contours, Martha and the Vandellas, Marvin Gaye, and the Spinners. The Four Tops weren't even at Motown then. The Supremes weren't at Motown. Stevie Wonder wasn't even at Motown."

There's a wistful coda. Forty years ago, Ghani visited the Motown Museum in Detroit. As museum hours were about to end, he discovered that the woman locking up the place was Anna Gordy.

Ghani told Gordy how the Sensations had impressed Harvey Fuqua in their audition at that midtown Cleveland hotel decades earlier. She told Ghani Fuqua was "the No. 1 entertainment agent for Motown" at the time, scolding Ghani for not making the Detroit trip. Things might have turned out very differently, she suggested.

"That's what happened to a lot of us," says Larry Banks, a childhood friend of Ghani who sang with him in the El Deons. "We just weren't hungry enough."

LEVERAGING LOCAL TALENT

MOTOWN CERTAINLY HAD CLOUT. Chuck Brown, who owned the Saru label in Cleveland in the '70s, said everybody wanted to be like Motown; that's why he had such high hopes for the Ponderosa Twins + One, two sets of identical twins and a non-relative Brown groomed to be Cleveland's answer to the Jackson Five. While Brown said the Twins + One did well locally, they never went truly nationwide. The twins were Keith and Kirk Gardner and Alvin and Alfred Pelham. The + One was Ricky Spicer.

"The O'Jays talked me into putting together a record company because at that time Motown was jumping big and we were only 165 miles from Detroit and they had local talent around here," said Brown, a soft-spoken, silver-haired bail bondsman.

Spicer says that if the Jackson 5 hadn't been around, "we would have been the next one," the kiddie group to go global.

Produced and arranged by the O'Jay Bobby Massey, the Ponderosa Twins + One released an album and five singles; the first single, a remake of Sam Cooke's "You Send Me," sold well in the Midwest, and the group toured, opening for the likes of James Brown and sharing bills with the O'Jays. As Spicer grew up, however, he grew disillusioned. And his voice changed.

"When you're a little kid, you only get to see the fun of it, you just want to sing," says Spicer. "Then it becomes a job and you can't go out and play because these adults want you to practice because you got shows to do. You always have to go to rehearsal; although I never achieved the fame Michael Jackson did, I know the scene of being a child entertainer and what comes with that. First you're this, and once you're not that anymore you're easily pushed aside and another little kid'll come in for you. We just kind of broke up after two hot years."

THE SOUR SMELL OF SUCCESS

THE ONLY CLEVELAND ACTS to make a big splash on Motown were Edwin Starr and the Dazz Band. And in both cases, success was fleeting and bittersweet.

Starr, a Tennessee native whose real name was Charles Edwin Hatcher, grew up in Cleveland and made his memorable pseudonym riding the psychedelic-political wave that swept Motown all the way to number one with his classic protest song "War." Other Starr hits include "25 Miles" and "Agent Double-O-Soul." But Starr, a child prodigy in Cleveland's Futuretones, eventually broke away from Motown. Gordy's operation folded Starr into its stable after purchasing Starr's original label, Ric-Tic, a subsidiary of Ed Wingate's Golden World, in 1968. (The Funk Brothers, incidentally, moonlighted for Ric-Tic as the San Remo Strings even as they were contracted to Gordy. This did not make Berry Gordy happy.)

According to Andrew Hamilton, a Cleveland journalist whose sister was

Hatcher's high-school girlfriend, Starr was a major figure at Ric-Tic and Golden World. When Gordy bought those labels from Detroit numbers man Wingate, he "bought" Starr, too, and at "Motown he was just a peon," Hamilton says.

Hatcher joined the Army under-age in 1960, and when he re-entered civilian life two years later, he tried to rejuvenate the Futuretones. Besides Hatcher on vocals, the group included Julius Roberts, bass; Otis Harris and Augustus Hawkins, saxophones; Clancy "Brownie" Wiley, drums; and Russell Evans, guitar.

The Futuretones couldn't muster a second wind, however, so in 1963, Hatcher hooked up with Hammond organist Bill Doggett, who was passing through Cleveland looking for a vocalist. Don Briggs, who managed the Bill Doggett Combo, came up with the name Edwin Starr, merging Hatcher's middle name with a twist on "star."

After several years with Doggett, Starr signed with Ric-Tic Records, the Wingate label that spawned his first hit, the James Bond takeoff "Agent Double-O-Soul." Starr also waxed several ballads for Ric-Tic. But when Gordy bought Ric-Tic, he began to bend Starr to Motown's image, signing him to his Gordy label and releasing such albums as the tough *25 Miles* and the duet curio, *Just We Two*. It wasn't until 1970, when modernist producer Norman Whitfield laid Starr's urgent vocals over a track originally recorded by the Temptations, that Starr became forever identified with "War," one of the earliest and grittiest antiwar songs.

Roberts and sax man Hawkins joined Starr's touring

THE O'JAYS

Promotional glossy, cropped for newspaper publishing, with original O'Jays members Eddie Levert, Walter Williams, Bobby Massey and, William Powell. The group was inducted into the Rock and Roll Hall of Fame in 2005, one of the few Cleveland soul groups to achieve breakout success.

band briefly in the late '70s. Roberts finally quit the Starr organization in 1979 after recording a disco album with him for 20th Century Fox in Los Angeles. Futuretones guitarist Evans hooked up with the O'Jays, Roberts eventually joined Harvey and the Phenomenals, and Hawkins took up with the Dynamic Sounds, a funk group he renamed S.O.U.L. (Sounds of Unity and Love). Both Roberts and Hawkins have passed.

Hamilton said Starr "hated Motown records. In fact, when he was still alive, that was a subject he would not even talk about."

"They put him on the back burner," Hawkins said of Motown's treatment of Starr. "If you weren't hot, they didn't want you in the building."

When the Futuretones visited "Hitsville USA" in '63 or '64, all the group had to offer was a tape, Hawkins said; the presentation was amateur. Berry Gordy "had a serious music business machine," he added. "We were out of their league. They were taking a break when we pulled up, and we must have looked like the Beverly Hillbillies. Diana Ross had her nose up in the air."

DAZZLING AND DESPERATE

THE DAZZ BAND EXPERIENCED a deeper, more damaging snub. Theirs is a story of record industry politics, conflicted management, and financial chicanery.

Led by saxophonist Bobby Harris and guitarist Mike Calhoun and anchored by the bass and drums of brothers Michael and Isaac Wiley, this 10-piece "ultrafunk" horn band started as Bell Telefunk in 1974. By the end of the decade, it had made two records for 20th Century Fox, the first as Kinsman Dazz, the second as simply Dazz. Vocalist Philip Bailey of Earth Wind & Fire produced the first after top choice Marvin Gaye took sick and begged off; Tommy Vicari and Pat Glasser helmed the second.

The Motown hookup coincided with the demise of 20th Century Fox, and the newly named Dazz Band scored hits with Motown until it left the label in 1985. Its biggest smash was "Let It Whip," a 1982 number that earned a Grammy for best rhythm and blues song of the year in 1983. *Keep It Live*, the album featuring "Let It Whip," was certified platinum for sales of more than 500,000 units. It reached number 14 on *Billboard*'s pop charts and hung there for 34 weeks. It also topped the magazine's rhythm and blues charts for five weeks.

The acclaim didn't last, and the band eventually fell apart despite a promising beginning and striking success. Management issues were critical.

Sonny Jones and Ray Calabrese, aka Sun-Ray Management, were the original managers. Jones owned the Kinsman Grill, where the band got its start. When Calabrese brought Joe Simone into Sun-Ray, Simone's $10,000 investment made him the dominant player—and Calabrese lost authority. "Joe listened to nobody," Calabrese said. "From that point on, I opposed almost any decision that was made." To little avail.

Jones died in the mid-'80s, Simone in the early '90s.

A man of acid wit, Calabrese said the basic problem was that Simone signed separate contracts with each band member and then indulged them. In addition, Progress Records, the Highland Heights, Ohio company Simone owned, distributed Motown records. Even when Progress lost a major account, Simone continued to pay the Dazz Band players. Calabrese

> **YOU'RE LOOKING AT THE GRAMMY ON YOUR MANTEL, AND YOU CAN'T PAY TO HEAT IT.**

said he thinks the Dazz Band should have worked more and subsequently sold more records.

"It wasn't my position to find them work," he said. "My opposition to the payroll was that this was a company I worked for. Why would I want to see a company I worked for drained?"

The economics and politics grew bleaker. In 1979, Progress lost A&M Records, a $3 million account. That same year, Mike Lushka, vice president of sales at Motown, was fired and replaced by Jay Lasker. Simone was anti-Lasker, the wrong position to take, particularly since Simone owed Motown money in connection with its distribution arrangement.

In 1983, when the Motown 25th Anniversary Special aired, the Dazz Band wasn't invited to participate, "and we'd just come off a gold record and a Grammy," lamented Calabrese. "The money we owed them consumed the profit." He also was convinced Motown kept Dazz off the 25th anniversary extravaganza to punish it for Simone's allegiance to Lushka.

That same year, the Dazz Band and Simone were linked to the collapse of Cleveland Community Savings & Loan, the city's first Black-owned financial institution. The Federal Home Loan Bank Board closed the Lee Road institution, ordering the Federal Savings and Loan Insurance Corp. to transfer Cleveland Community Savings deposits to another savings association. A Federal Bureau of Investigation probe centered on four individuals and three corporations; among the latter was Simone's Progress Entertainment Corporation.

Progress "produces the Dazz Band, a chain of retail record stores and other entertainment related activities," said the November 10, 1983 *Call & Post*. The Dazz Band invested in Cleveland Community Savings, buying stock for $1,000 per share. In an article three weeks later, the Dazz Band's Bobby Harris told the paper band members had invested in Cleveland Community "to return some of the fame and fortune they have earned to the city that is their home." He said loans Simone received were unrelated to the stock purchases. Simone never went to jail in connection with the scandal, according to Calabrese.

After the band left Motown, it recorded first for Geffen, then for RCA, then for lesser labels. It was a long, slow fade to black. Bassist-vocalist Mike Wiley, a Dazz original, fatally shot himself, said Calabrese, probably because of drugs and depression.

"You're looking at the Grammy on your mantel in your house," Calabrese says, "and you can't pay to heat it."

The Dazz Band declined for multiple reasons, some personal, some specific to the record business of the late '80s, which was churning through labels, agencies and distribution models. An earlier Invisible Soul talent didn't let bad fortune rule his career.

DAZZ BAND

BIG BEN RECORDS / LOS ANGELES HOSTED MOTOWN ARTISTS IN STORE PROMOTION CAMPAIGN ON SATURDAY AUGUST 14, 1982

A classic 8"x10" promo photo during the ascendancy of one of Cleveland's soul groups that leapt to international acclaim. Nearly 25 different musicians, past and present, claim Dazz Band ancestry.

Up Front and ON TIME

Eddie Baccus Sr. and Lee Sykes were singular utility players, delivering pop-rock, pop-jazz and straight jazz out of a storefront on 105 that drew the best players in town. Talk about a Dynamic Duo!

FOR MOST OF US, A DIAGNOSIS OF IMPENDING blindness would be a kind of death sentence. Not so for Eddie Baccus Sr., Cleveland's master of the Hammond B-3 organ, a signature keyboard of Cleveland's soul scene.

To Baccus and his partner, the drummer Lester Sykes, East 105th Street near Euclid Avenue was their preferred place to play. This was before 105 was the origin of a major infrastructure project dedicated to economic development in Cleveland's blighted urban core. Now, it's the Opportunity Corridor. Then, it was a different zone of opportunity.

Baccus and Sykes spent part of the '60s working that zone. The Dynamic Duo staked their claim to local fame in the front window of Jack Gould's Esquire Lounge at 10530 Euclid. The marquee position they occupied there in 1964 and 1965 drew better than well.

They also played many other places, including after-hours joints like Johnny's Round Table on Quincy Avenue. And early that decade, Baccus stayed—and performed—at the 250-room Majestic Hotel at 55th and Central.

"You could stay at the Majestic Hotel for probably $15-$20 a week," he said. "Most of the Black entertainers, that's where they stayed."

"We used to play some of everything," Sykes said in a joint interview with

Eddie Baccus

Baccus in 2012. "We played Top 40, stuff by the Spinners, everything that was out."

The venues were plentiful and the music spanned everything from the Delta blues of Robert Lockwood Jr. to the far-out jazz of Omnibus, a big band put together by up-and-coming tenor saxophonist Ernie Krivda. The '60s and '70s, rocked as they were by racial strife, were musically turbulent in the best sense.

Sykes and Baccus were so busy they had to move Baccus's organ from club to club five, six times a week. "From Kinsman Grill to Mardi Gras to Midway Lake, we moved the Hammond a lot, just me and him," Sykes said.

Baccus was born in 1936, Sykes in 1941.

Baccus, a North Carolina native who went blind at an early age, attended the Ohio State School for the Blind in Columbus, where he met fellow student Roland Kirk. Baccus dropped out of school to work in Kirk's trio, and arrived in Cleveland at the dawn of the '60s. Kirk, who would soon adopt the name "Rahsaan," was a jazz genius who could play three wind instruments at a time—and not necessarily in unison.

"I played with him for about a year in Columbus and different places, but then I started having a lot of dreams about how I was the only one in the family who didn't graduate," Baccus said. So Baccus, who suffered from a degenerative eye disease that affected half of the 10 children in his family, went back to Columbus, graduated in 1958, and shortly after began performing in Kirk's group along with Charles Crosby, a drummer Baccus would incorporate into one of his own combos.

Home to the Roland Kirk Trio, six nights a week, was Eddie Bogan's Club 100 at 10020 Euclid. For a time, the club became Baccus's home away from home; he learned B-3 tricks from an organist who performed there named Melvin Jones, and he would practice at Club 100 every day. (The singular, protean Kirk, who had been playing in Cleveland since 1957, suffered a debilitating stroke in 1975 and died in 1977. He was 41. Baccus died January 23, 2022.)

In 1958 and 1959, Baccus played piano behind Kirk, but by 1961, he'd switched to organ. In 1962, Baccus recorded an album, *Feel Real*, in Chicago for Smash, a subsidiary of the Mercury Records label; Baccus plays organ exclusively on it—it features two Kirk tunes—and Crosby plays drums on several tracks. Baccus said he also recorded a blues number called "Bacon and Eggs" at Boddie Recording with Lockwood Jr. and Crosby on drums; it was never released.

Both Sykes and Baccus waxed nostalgic about other gigs—with Bill Doggett, a rhythm-and-blues organist who also worked with Cleveland vocalist Charles Hatcher before

THEY PUT A GUN ON ME FIRST BECAUSE I WAS THE GUY STANDING AT THE DOOR WAITING TO GET PAID. THEY PUT A GUN TO EDDIE'S HEAD.

he made a name for himself as Edwin Starr; with Willie "Face" Smith, the great arranger and alto saxophonist; and popular band leaders Jimmy Landers and Jimmy St. Clair.

Sykes is a Cleveland native who grew up on Parmelee Avenue between 105th and St. Clair when it was "a Jewish neighborhood, where all the rich people lived."

"My parents were one of the first Black families on our street," he said. "Larry Doby of the Cleveland Indians, the first Black to play in the American League, stayed there because it was a good neighborhood, the Shaker Heights for Blacks at the time; that's why they called it the Gold Coast."

Sykes first demonstrated his talent by playing on tables at Miles Standish Elementary School (now Michael R. White Elementary School) on East 92nd Street. He began to play professionally when he was under age, at the Hound Dog's Den, a blues bar on Kinsman at 116th Street.

"The first artist I played with was John Lee Hooker," he said, namechecking one of the most compelling and influential electric bluesmen. "I was 16 years old and I had to stay on stage," Sykes recalled. "They were giving me so much ginger ale I got high drinking ginger ale."

Before he joined up with Baccus, Sykes was playing r&b in Tommy O'Neal and the Thunderbirds, performing at the Wheel Lounge on Lee Road near Miles and at the Harlem Club on Cedar Avenue at 100th Street across from Cedar Gardens. In 1964, Sykes left O'Neal's band to play jazz with Melvin Jones, that very same organist who helped Baccus out when Baccus was still apprenticing. Sykes soon after found his musical soulmate, quitting Jones's group to work with Baccus. The two traveled to gigs in a big V8, Sykes' 1964 Plymouth Sports Fury.

Things could get dicey. Both recalled an incident in the late '60s when Cleveland detectives broke the plate glass window at the Esquire in search of a waitress they suspected of prostitution.

"They were drunk and the owners there knew them," Sykes said. "They put a gun on me first because I was the guy standing at the door waiting to get paid. They put a gun to Eddie's head." The detectives took the two to the Fifth District police station on Euclid off Chester and kept them a while, ultimately bringing them back to the Esquire.

"That was when I knew it was time to get out of town," Sykes said. "I didn't really want to play with Bill Doggett, but I needed a change."

The two also were for hire, occasionally backing Motown singer Gladys Knight and more often working for Kim Tolliver, a Cleveland vocalist known for her charisma and fashion sense. Among the places they played behind Tolliver: Don King's Midway Lake Park in Orwell, which King turned into a training camp for the boxer Mike Tyson in the 1980s.

Baccus had other jobs, too. In the latter part of the '60s and into the '70s, he gigged with white saxophonist Dave O'Rourke at the Corner Tavern, King's nightclub at 78th Street and Cedar.

In the '60s and early '70s, Baccus and Sykes would play Midway Lake on weekends, returning to Cleveland to

Starring Eddie Baccus, applauded Organ Star & Lester Sykes, King of the Skins.

THIS FRIDAY AND SATURDAY

THE DYNAMIC DUO

KITCHEN FOR LEASE
CALL FOR APPOINTMENT

DAILY HAPPY HOUR 4-6 p.m.

ROOMS 9 95 up

60 Attractive Rooms, reasonably priced. You can now apply for our PREFERRED RATE CARD, good Sunday thru Thursday.

McCALL'S MOTOR INN

14660 Euclid Ave. 681-8500

perform Sunday night and every night of the following week. The Esquire Lounge, the Kinsman Grill, the Mardi Gras, and the Player's Den were regular weeknight gigs. But the Esquire was their favorite.

"We had the best jam session in town at the Esquire Lounge," said Baccus.

"Sometimes we had 15 horn players on the set, guys so good that we had to start playing more," Sykes added. "We gave a lot of people breaks. That's why our gigs were so good, because there were so many musicians." Among artists they backed, mostly at the Esquire: nationally known saxophonists Lou Donaldson, George Coleman, and George Adams, and Jimmy Scott, that singular, androgynous singer.

"We were always ourselves," Sykes said. "We backed up singers, but they worked with us. We were always our own package."

The Esquire was often standing room only when the Dynamic Duo were on the case, "back when Cleveland was cool," Sykes says. "All the big time musicians who were recording artists used to come in and see us when they'd be in town."

If Sykes and Baccus laid down the grooves that caught the ears of Invisible Soul musicians, a Glenville merchant delivered the look.

8 MAN *Talk,* MAN *Walks*

Chuck Avner made a career of selling high-style clothing to Blacks, whether common men or celebrities. His move east out of Glenville was a tough but necessary decision, reflecting the times and the man.

WHEN CLEVELAND'S GLENVILLE neighborhood exploded in late July 1968, the fate of one of its last white-owned businesses hung in the balance. In 2011, I interviewed the owner of that business. I came away with appreciation for the role he played in Cleveland's soul scene.

Fortified by his Army discharge papers and a diploma from Western Reserve University, Chuck Avner put his business degree and expansive personality to work at Ritz Men's Wear, a shop in Cleveland's rapidly changing East Side. Over a few years after World War II, the transition from a mostly white to integrated to a mostly Black neighborhood played out in an era and city ill-equipped to handle so seismic a shift.

Still, Avner worked to remain above the racial fray. Unlike many whites of his times, he was more than accepting of Blacks. He was an ardent fan of theirs, and he considered Black culture and sense of style superior. But, as he learned more about the retail clothing business in 1950s Cleveland, his disillusionment grew.

Avner realized that at best, Black customers were being cheated—they were sold inferior and irregular products at premium prices. "A friend of mine who had a store at 105th and Euclid wouldn't let a Black guy try on a pair of pants," Avner told me.

After he learned the retail clothing business, he decided he wanted to be his own boss, be successful, and sell fashionable clothes at a fair price to those who needed and appreciated style: Black customers. "They're the only ones who had taste in clothes," Avner said. But his white peers ridiculed him for his progressive views.

"I'm one of these guys people used to call 'nigger lover,'" he said.

Undaunted, Avner launched his retail empire in Glenville in 1952, nicking his store's name from cartoonist Jimmy Hatlo, creator of the long-running comic strip "They'll Do It Every Time." From the start, Hatlo's 5th Avenue Men's Shop at 1037 East 105th Street, like its suburban successor ManTalk, was a palpable hit.

Avner worked the media well. He also entered into commercial relationships with prominent Black businessmen. He became friends with numbers kingpin Arthur "Little Brother" Drake and restaurateur Ulysses S. Dearing, founder of Dearing's Restaurants, an inner-city chain.

MUSIC AND MURK

EARLY IN HIS HATLO'S phase, Avner bonded with Drake, who owned the Cafe Tia Juana with his wife, Catherine, and their white partner, William "Willie" Hoge. In its heyday, the Tia Juana was one of the hottest jazz supper clubs in the nation, showcasing the likes of Nat "King" Cole, Billie Holiday, Miles Davis, and Charlie Parker. It was on Massie Avenue, two doors north of Hatlo's.

Where Avner went into business to level the racial playing field, the Drakes launched the Tia Juana in 1947 as a jazz sanctuary for interracial audiences; their motivation stemmed from an incident in which Catherine Drake was refused admittance to a club while a white companion went right on in. "Little Brother" was fearless, said Avner, recalling a confrontation between Drake and a famous Cleveland gangland figure: "I saw him challenge Shondor Birns, and Shondor Birns was a muscle guy with the mob, an enforcer."

As Jews fled Glenville's Gold Coast and Blacks moved in, the racial divide and the lawlessness attending the numbers racket began to hurt the Tia Juana, famous for its exotic decor and its musical offerings but increasingly disreputable for drug busts, stabbings and gunshots.

The Drakes were having personal trouble, too, and the numbers—the underworld precursor to the state lottery—went too high-profile for comfort. Drake and Hoge went to jail in 1949, serving four years on a blackmail charge connected to their boring in on rival policy houses.

Drake died of heart disease in January 1956. His funeral, a gathering of Fleetwoods, DeVilles, and Eldorados, drew the gilded, the garish, and the sketchy from all over the country. Avner was a pallbearer. A 125-car procession from St. Timothy Missionary Baptist church brought Drake from East 71st Street and Carnegie Avenue to his final resting place in Highland Park Cemetery.

Avner also had a ground-floor connection to another storied club, Winston Willis's Jazz Temple at Mayfield Road and Euclid.

"I GREW UP IN GLENVILLE, AND WE HAD AFRICAN-AMERICAN BUSINESSES ON 105, JUST FLOURISHING."

Like the Tia Juana, the Jazz Temple was designed to be a club for interracial audiences. Like the Tia Juana, it was associated with violence. And, like the Tia Juana, jazz greats like "Cannonball" Adderley played there, as did bebop (and then some) legends Miles Davis, Herbie Hancock, Dizzy Gillespie, and John Coltrane. Jazz Temple owner Willis knew Davis personally. He also knew about floor covering, having come up through his father's floor covering business.

The Jazz Temple was down the street from Little Italy, a clannish community where restaurants often refused to serve Blacks. The Temple's reputation for integration didn't sit well with the immediate neighborhood, and Willis and his girlfriend, Charlene Hurd, became the subjects of death threats. A dynamite explosion in 1963 led to costly repairs, but the club persisted. Still, the number of threats grew, culminating in 1965, when a bomb demolished the building. It never came back.

Avner had an inside story about the Jazz Temple. It's murky but suggestive. The people who put the club together wanted him to be a partner in that risky, progressive venture.

"I said I don't want to be a partner but I'll help you get a liquor permit," Avner recalled telling Willis. "You got to do one thing for me."

In exchange for his permit power, Avner wanted help at the Glenville Neighborhood Development Corp., where he was a board member. "These guys installed tiled floors. We needed a tile floor. We needed painting, we needed a lot of stuff," he said.

"I'll get this (permit) for you," Avner said, "but you guys have to lay the floor at our Glenville headquarters in payment. I got the tile. I wanted the labor. After I got them the permit from the city, these *mamzers* did not do it. I cussed them up and down, I called them every name in the book and they threatened me with my life. They were bad guys, but you have to understand, I've been through a lot of shit in my life.

"The fact that I'm alive today, God watches over me."

SETTING THE TRENDS

AVNER WOULD STOP BY Leo's Casino maybe once a week to gab with Freddie Arrington, the MC there, and owners Leo Frank and Jules Berger. He recalled a special gathering at the basement club.

Avner was sharing a table with Eddie Levert, Frank, and Eddie O'Jay, a disc jockey at AM station WABQ. Levert headed the Mascots, a group from Canton that was performing at Leo's. Name change came up.

"Eddie O'Jay says, Why don't you call yourself the O'Jays?" O'Jay told Levert. That's how the name started, Avner recalled. "Eddie O'Jay managed the group before Leo did, and then Leo came into the picture. They liked the name the O'Jays, and they used it."

While the original O'Jays were not Man Talk customers, Eddie's sons Gerald and Sean were. Avner also catered to whites craving an edge in their look.

"I wanted to open up a Mod shop," he said. "Mod was coming in but you couldn't get Mod clothes here, you had to go to England." At first, his partners resisted. But one day, as the Man Talk brain trust was buying clothes wholesale at the Versaille Motor Inn, a hotel at 2901 Euclid that catered to entertainers, a friend wheeled in a rack of Mod garments.

Avner was dazzled by these American-made copies of English Edwardian apparel. Sharing the dazzle was a longhair in skinny jeans who overheard the conversation among the Man Talk buyers and chimed in, saying he supported Avner's vision. He said he was from Flint, Michigan and his group was always looking for clothes. The man was Terry Knight, a regular performer at Leo's with his Terry Knight Revue, which featured the arrangements of Tom Baker and the saxophone of Ernie Krivda.

Avner went all-in on Mod.

"I hit a jackpot," Avner said. "My store was the place to buy clothes. Man Talk was packed. The kids loved my clothes."

Knight, of course, hit much bigger pay dirt, first with Terry Knight and the Pack, then big-time with Grand Funk Railroad.

Avner sold the hippest threads of the day to local residents, national musicians and celebrities of all stripes. It's hard to believe that less than 10 years after the peak of Avner's retail dream he would find himself holed up in his store after hours facing a crowd of angry looters.

Making the situation even more dire was the appearance of a Cleveland policeman, brandishing a shotgun and telling Avner, "I'm going to kill these Black motherfuckers."

RISING FROM THE ASHES

WHEN HE LAUNCHED HIS clothing business in 1952, Avner couldn't have anticipated how sour the racial situation would become in the following decade. But he wasn't surprised when rioters virtually destroyed Hatlo's, his flagship store in Glenville, in July 1968.

"The gates were ripped down, the windows were broken, half the store was gone," Avner said, fuming at the horrific memory. "The police stopped angry people, and there were plenty of angry people. I heard people call me names. Then I heard other people say, Why did it happen to him? I have no animosity toward what happened. The riots had to happen in Cleveland. They had to happen in this country, because the Blacks were suppressed. You can't take what white America did to the Blacks. It was inevitable."

As he built his mini-empire, Avner's boisterous personality and love of the honest hustle colored his business relationships, but his pragmatic side didn't allow for self-delusion. In a mostly Black, increasingly strident inner-city Cleveland neighborhood, Avner knew that success for a white retailer faced long odds. He certainly never imagined that his commitment to his business would jeopardize his survival.

Nevertheless, pure survival dominated Avner's mind that moment in July 1968. The storefront of his stylish shop lay trashed on the sidewalk. Much of his prized, fashionable goods was looted or destroyed. He stood, horrified, and shoulder-to-shoulder with an armed cop who seemed more intent on killing Blacks than protecting Avner's business.

The overwhelming presence of force, mutual fear, or cool-headed intervention—it's unclear exactly how a deadly outcome was avoided in that place, that night. The police officer, members of the mob, and Avner himself emerged unscathed, at least physically, from that confrontation in Hatlo's 5th Avenue Men's Shop. But so much else died in Glenville—and Cleveland's soul—in the years to follow.

Shops were boarded up, often reopening just long enough for owners to pack up and ship out. There was destruction, and loss of community. Some say Glenville still hasn't come back. Drive 105 and the evidence is clear.

Cleveland Councilman Kevin Conwell reflects on the loss.

"I grew up in Glenville, and we had African-American businesses on 105, just flourishing," he said. "The riots destroyed a lot of the infrastructure in the community, and people started leaving."

Man Talk was high, hip fashion.

AVNER'S GOAL: "TO PROVE THAT BLACKS WITH THEIR FASHION SENSE WILL APPRECIATE QUALITY. THE BLACKS ARE SO FORWARD-FASHION OVER THE WHITES."

PERSISTENCE PAYS OFF

AFTER THAT DEVASTATING RUCKUS, Avner was one of the neighborhood fixtures who never came back. He closed up business, first his satellite operation on Superior Avenue, and then his gem on 105. Hatlo's store had felt like a jail to Avner years earlier as he logged crushing hours to build a business that paid off for him and the community. But now Avner found himself trapped in a truer kind of jail—he was scared to open his shop and scared to leave it. Literally, fear had him coming and going.

So Avner did what successful people of every era do: adapt, evolve, and if necessary, migrate. He took his gifts of fashion, business, and personal style east. His destination was just a little over three miles, but for Avner it opened up a whole new world. His first suburban store, Man Talk, opened in 1968 in Cleveland Heights in sleek, climate-controlled Severance Center, the first enclosed shopping mall in Ohio. Another Man Talk opened about 10 miles south in Randall Park Mall, touted then as "The Biggest Mall in All the World."

His goal "was to prove that Blacks with their fashion sense will appreciate quality," Avner said. "That's what my premise was going into business. I only carried quality merchandise, first-quality. I never cheated them, but I didn't give myself away. The Blacks are so forward-fashion over the whites. I think there's a parity now," he told me.

Chuck Avner died in 2012, not much more than a year after we talked.

I came to regard him as part of the fabric of Invisible Soul, a figure who also served as a cultural bridge. He was someone in the wings, a background character who in effect helped put a production together. A performer has to look good, and Avner knew how to make that happen.

He made a point of selling to Blacks when other whites refused to. His taste, his appetite for music, and his openness to fashion no matter the showman's color made things easier for the men in the spotlight.

Avner (with a saxophone) retained his flair for marketing with music when he moved east to Severance Center Mall.

INVISIBLE SOUL MEN

More than one Black Cleveland performer laments the lack of a promoter or manager persistent enough to take a local group nationwide. There were promoters like Syd Friedman and—wearing one of his many hats—the multifaceted Lou Ragland. But for the most part, entertainers connected to Cleveland's soul scene profiled here worked their circuits on their own, without a third-party agent or promoter. Because of the difficulty of marketing and booking your own act outside the local area, few of these "self-promoters" were successful in breaking out.

I wish I'd interviewed more women for this book; at the same time, the four men I focus on next stand out for their doggedness, the pleasure they took in performing well into old age, and their versatility. All were born in Cleveland. All have, or had, great affection for the city that accorded them star status. But all have wistful wisdom to share as well.

9 *Preaching the* GOSPEL OF SOUL

More than 60 years on, Art Blakey sings soul with a hot, much younger band and lifts people up with his gospel stylings. Lord, how the man smiles!

ARTHUR BLAKEY WAS BORN TO SING. TODAY, at the age of 82, the charismatic Cleveland vocalist still brings the house down. House of worship or nightclub, doesn't matter. His voice takes you home.

The vocal bug bit Art Blakey early. He and his buddies from Thomas Edison Junior High School seemed to pull music out of the atmosphere. In that era, that's what radio felt like: magical.

The boys scoured the AM dial for the harmonies of groups like the Andrews Sisters and the Ink Spots. They listened to Grand Ole Opry broadcasts from Ryman Auditorium in Nashville, adding country flavor to the influences that make Art Blakey such a compelling singer. And at the dawn of the 1950s, a decade in which vocals ruled and music became a democratizing force, everybody listened to Alan Freed, aka "Moondog," the WJW disc jockey credited with promoting the first rock and roll concert.

Affection for country and western music might seem incongruous for a Black entertainer. But both c&w and soul music share earthy and melodic features, and they feel organic. There was no need to segregate the genres when both were ascendant, each of them complementary. They blended smoothly in the songs of "Bronze Buckaroo" Herb Jeffries, a Black cowboy singer who starred in sepia Westerns. In more modern times, Charley Pride, the award-winning Black c&w star, carried on Jeffries' tradition.

In the '50s, Perry Como gave way to Little Richard. Pat Boone bleached Fats Domino. Incongruities smoothed over as Black and white audiences converged in musical taste, creating the mainstream, the umbrella, we know as rock and roll.

In the '50s and '60s, every neighborhood had a singing group, Blakey said. Jazz and blues groups drew fans to clubs on Cleveland's East Side, and doo-wop began to morph into more instrumentally oriented rhythm and blues in groups like Bobby Womack's Valentinos and the Futuretones, the city's first self-contained band. The vocalist Sonny Turner, who would become lead singer in the Platters, began in Cleveland's Metrotones, a doo-wop group with a local hit called "Skitter Skatter" in the mid-50s. "There was a wealth of talent, and you had to be decent to even talk about getting a gig around here with all the different people coming in," Blakey says.

In the early '60s, Motown, too, cast both spell and shadow. Local musicians frequently were hired to accompany Motown stars performing in Cleveland. Blakey met Stevie Wonder at Cleveland Arena and played behind stars like Mary Wells and Marvin Gaye. Detroit and Cleveland, just three hours apart, crossed currents all the time. But while Blakey was aware of the allure of bigger markets, for him Cleveland was always the prize he could enjoy.

ART'S START

AN ONLY CHILD BORN on March 19, 1941 to musical parents, Blakey grew up in Cleveland's Central District, exercising his vocal cords in junior choir at Second Mount Sinai Baptist Church on East 75th Street. If church was his way into gospel, radio—still AM, still largely segregated—was a school of greater bandwidth, introducing him to a stimulating hodge-podge of styles.

"Back in those days, we didn't have a lot of radio stations that played rhythm and blues, so when it came Sunday morning I used to love to hear the old gospel," he says. "Your Hit Parade" played the hits of the day, Paul Whiteman—a white man—was king of the band leaders, and in the '50s, jazz was still a form of popular music: "I remember listening to the radio at night and hearing that Billie Holiday died," Blakey says.

Rhythm and blues sprouted shortly after Blakey absorbed the sounds of the Ink Spots, the Mills Brothers, and some of his favorite harmonizers, Roy Rogers and the Sons of the Pioneers. Groups named after cars and birds—the Cadillacs, the El Dorados, the Flamingos, the Edsels, the Orioles—were all the rage, and all featured that creamy blend Blakey craved. Based on a cappella, doo-wop reigned in the early '50s, morphing into rhythm and blues when vocal combos evolved to add instruments.

Assembling voices is easy when music is all around; it's mostly a matter of simple addition. Harmonizing is far more difficult, however, involving selecting different but complementary voices, then blending them live in a song. Far more difficult, but done well, the effect would amplify the sound of the group.

"I was in my yard one day and heard some guys singing on the corner," Blakey recalls. "I was hanging around with my little buddies because I was scared of the bullies, and when I heard this harmony, I said, Nah, I ain't staying in this yard." When he found that group of harmonizing singers, he also found direction for his musical career.

At the time, it seemed every neighborhood boasted at least one singing group. The image of the street corner symphony became a kind of cliché, in Broadway plays like *West Side Story* or even Hollywood hits like *Rocky*.

Blakey paints the picture. "That's what we did: stand around, harmonize, and play basketball. When I heard these guys I went down, I started singing lead, they started singing background, and it sounded good. Then I started singing background and found out I knew harmony just from hearing it.

"With the harmony, when it's there, you know it's right."

His pals, however, couldn't follow a pattern as well as he could. "They would try but they really could not sing," Blakey says. "When I got up there, all I had to do was fill in. The first notes would establish who's singing what." Harmonic discipline was a natural for Blakey. It would place him in good stead when he formed the Hesitations, his most successful musical venture.

"We weren't nothin'," Blakey says of those youthful days. "We had no name. We were together all the time. What got us started singing was our friends. By the time we hit junior high we were doing contests, making a name for ourselves."

YOU LIKE US? WE'LL BE BACK NEXT WEEK—BUT THIS TIME WE'LL GET PAID.

Not only did Blakey make lifelong friends through music, he initiated professional relationships that led him to perform with various groups into the 21st century. Pinpointing start and end dates for groups of that period is challenging. Blakey gives the effort a heroic try.

His first group included William Carter and Robert Middlebrook, who would become latter-day Hesitations, and Lou Ragland, who would work with Blakey in several bands. They would rehearse from the time school let out to late at night.

One day, a woman who would greatly influence Blakey caught the fledgling entertainers singing along with "Dance!" outside a restaurant in Cleveland's Central District. When Blakey and his pals continued singing well after the song ended, Gloria Jean Brown thought the Coasters tune seemed really long. But it left an impression.

Managed by the enterprising Brown, who also was an exotic dancer, Blakey's no-name combo tightened up, developing steps so smooth and harmonies so silken it was impossible to tell who was singing which part.

"She would win money off friends and other musicians who were around the Chitlin' Circuit," Blakey recalls. "She would tell them, 'You can walk around, you can listen, I guarantee you can't tell who's singing what note; the harmony was perfect.' She would not allow it any other way."

Making a mark didn't come easy in such a competitive club environment. Gigs regularly included a band, maybe a tap dancer, a solo singer, a singing group, a comedian. Blakey would not only sing, he and a friend did stand-up comedy.

It's hard for me to visualize toggling between balladeer and jokester, but Blakey and that era were all about versatility. Take a chance, pitch in, make a few extra bucks by doing more than one job, whatever it takes. Blakey's career rose in the waning days of burlesque, a performance art form as old as the saloon days of the American West. Born out of the need to assemble a lengthy program for an audience of mixed sensibilities, comic routines as long as 20 minutes or as brief as three or four gags were a staple of burlesque and other popular performances. Eventually, brief comedic bits in the form of banter would evolve. Musical performers would appear to take a break to engage in spontaneous commentary with the audience or band members. It made the performers more human and the performances more authentic, but most banter was highly scripted and rehearsed.

Of course, another reason for injecting comedy into burlesque and vaudeville shows was to distract the large portion of the male audience impatiently waiting for the striptease acts. While T and A was the main attraction for burlesque shows, scantily clad women assumed a secondary role in Cleveland's Invisible Soul scene.

Exotic, "shake" dancers were often on the bill and the shows were long and demanding. To recharge and jam, Blakey says that he—and many other Cleveland musicians—patronized an enchanting residence at 96th Street and Cedar Road known simply as Miss Rose's.

I can only imagine what Miss Rose's was like.

In the late '50s, Blakey and his group, now named the Orientals, barnstormed in a white 1952 Buick Roadmaster convertible, "riding down 55th or Cedar, and wherever they would have a bar, we would go in and do our show. For free.

"You like us?" the group would tell the proprietor. "We'll be back next week—but this time we'll get paid."

Getting paid was by no means a sure thing.

TIGHTENING UP

THERE WAS THAT TIME the Orientals returned to a bar they'd played gratis a week earlier. They were hoping to make money this second trip. When Gloria Brown went inside to scout it out, she saw the place was packed. But the bar owner wasn't willing to pay, so the Orientals went to one down the street, their fans right behind them. The Orientals would gain an adoring audience, and the club that wouldn't cough up $50 would lose a vibrant, hard-drinking audience for the night.

"I made more money with the Orientals than I did with anything else, even the Hesitations, for a while," Blakey says. Too bad the Orientals didn't record. Another wallflower in Cleveland's often too Invisible Soul landscape.

In August 1958, the Orientals won a battle of the bands at Prince Hall Masonic Temple. Brown told the *Call & Post* they owed their success to daily practice and a dedication to perfection. The singers credited their fan club officers: Renee Fell, president, and Barbara White, secretary. White would become key to the Invisible Soul infrastructure. Her styling and management of the Entertains, Harvey and the

Phenomenals, and other groups, among other bands, were essential to keeping the wheels turning.

Blakey's first name band was the Collegians, which included his friend, fellow former Sahib and latter-day Hesitation George Hendricks. The Collegians were so skilled that if one member was unavailable to perform, Blakey or Hendricks could fill in.

"In each group I got something that I didn't get from the other that helped me get better at my game," Blakey says.

By his late teens, Blakey was well on his way to a career as an entertainer. At the same time, he was a family man, with family obligations. Music always was more of a calling than a sideline, but performance gigs couldn't provide the steady income a household demands.

After graduating from high school, Blakey made a commitment. He became a nursing assistant and physical therapist. He also worked at Republic Steel for a spell, and spent 25 years on the road driving semis, making sure to get home every weekend.

Married three times, he is the father of 14 children by his first two wives. "I didn't get rich, but I kept my head above water," Blakey says.

TERRIFIC IN TURBANS

AS THE DECADE TURNED over, Blakey worked in two key groups, the Crown Imperials and the better-known Sahibs, who wore turbans in the style of "King of the Stroll" Chuck Willis. Collegians alumni James Dotson and Benny Butcher technically launched the Crown Imperials, but to Blakey, the evolution of one group into another attests to fluidity, one of the key attributes of Cleveland's slippery musical scene. For a time, several of Cleveland's vocal kingpins were legacy Sahibs.

Pinpointing that group's origin is next to impossible and, like the Orientals, the Sahibs never recorded. They would form, split up, reform, and quit; in one configuration or another, they made it to 1970, if only in name.

"All of us were the same group," Blakey says. "It was just about who were the ones who were together at the time. Most of those guys were also Crown Imperials."

I sense that bands defined themselves by the gig, or by one evening's challenge. Such was the changeable identity of Cleveland's Invisible Soul scene.

The Crown Imperials dueled the Sahibs in a battle of the bands at the Circle Theatre, where in the mid-50s Blakey caught his first rhythm and blues show, featuring Bo Diddley as headliner. "I came out of there and I was so overwhelmed, I said that was what I wanted to do, period," Blakey says, still Diddley-dazzled after all these years.

As a Crown Imperial, he says, he was on a bill with "Little" Stevie Wonder at the Cleveland Arena; Wonder was a very precocious youngster at the time, touring behind "Fingertips Part II." Blakey and Wonder would meet again when both appeared on a bill at the Uptown Theatre in Philadelphia.

On Saturday nights, the Circle Theatre presented the Hillbilly Jamboree, emceed by WERE-AM disc jockey Tommy Edwards. On Sundays, it presented rhythm and blues shows. Promoter Syd Friedman booked acts into the venue, highlighting local groups on Sundays. Friedman would end up managing one of those locals: the Wigs, featuring Blakey as lead singer, along with other alumni of the Crescents, a Cleveland doo-wop group that scored a local hit with the pretty "Julie" in 1956.

"The Crown Imperials versus the Sahibs was strange," Blakey says. That particular competition made him feel as if he was battling himself "because we had more of the old Sahibs and Collegians than the Sahibs had in their group."

The Sahibs won that test, prompting Crown Imperial William "Cosmo" Carter to defect to the victors, who at one time also included Lou Ragland, who went by the nickname "Ejoe," and Hendricks, who went by "Poochie." There were groups of greater skill, Blakey says, "but at the time we were also some of the cutest guys in the neighborhood. That helped a lot.

"That was a different era," he says. "We were like

gunslingers with voices. We were friends until we went on the stage; we went on stage to cut your throat. We had mutual respect for each other. I'm talking about the O'Jays, I'm talking about Bobby Womack, Edwin Starr. Those are the people we had to compete against. That was my neighborhood."

Blakey sang all over town. For an early-60s minute, he sang with the Flames (aka the Five Fabulous Flames), Harvey Hall's group. He also sang in the Rose Room of the Majestic Hotel, where Eddie Kendricks and Paul Williams worked before they left Cleveland for Detroit and became Temptations.

TUNING INTO LEO'S

BLAKEY EVEN BUSED TABLES at Leo's Casino for a while; he loved Leo Frank, who owned the Euclid Avenue club with Jules Berger. Blakey also helped that legendary venue secure a band that could back Motown artists road-testing their acts in Cleveland.

Take this run in fall 1965. The headliner was Motown's Mary Wells, and the Wigs opened, from November 11 to November 14. The backup band was problematic.

"We told Leo he needed a band for this show. We told him we had a band, but it was a jazz band," he recalls. A jazz band of peculiar provenance.

Former Crescent Albert Banks worked with Blakey in the Wigs, Syd Friedman's retrofit of the Crescents. The Wigs were outfitted in colonial attire as a Black "answer" to the Beatles. Banks had come up with that jazz band, headed by a man named Monk Nervous, for Leo's, but the jazzers couldn't lock down the groove. Blakey came up with an alternative that was more than effective.

Long after the heyday of Cleveland's soul scene passed, Art Blakey still rocks a classy suit. (Carlo Wolff)

"When we went to Leo's, the band would play jazz beautifully in their part of the set," he says. "But when it came time for Mary Wells and us to do our show… jazz musicians can't play rhythm and blues. They didn't have that spark and feel, especially back then. Rhythm and blues were getting a little more intricate at the time. The show was so dull we were getting what we call 'courtesy claps.'"

After a few nights, it was time for a change. Monk Nervous was out, the Futuretones were in. Blakey introduced Frank and Berger to the Futuretones. A footnote: Mary Wells, who became famous for hits such as "My Guy" and "You Beat Me to the Punch," had a direct Cleveland connection. For 10 years, she was married to Cecil Womack, a member of the Valentinos and the brother of Bobby Womack of "It's All Over Now" fame.

More than a footnote: the Wigs was the first band Blakey recorded with. Waxed in 1964 at Cleveland Recording, the Wigs' Golden Crest 45, "You're Sweeter Than Wine/Chicken Switch," fetches a pretty price; as of March 2023, the single was for sale at recording rarity website Discogs for about $750. Producer Carl Maduri and promoter Friedman took composer credit, which they shouldn't have, Blakey says. Maduri "wasn't even there for the recording when we put all of that together—the band, everything." Blakey was lead singer, and the split harmonies of the four front-line vocalists gave the illusion of a larger group.

ANCIENT HISTORY

BLAKEY HAS PERFORMED IN at least eight groups including the Wigs, the Collegians, the Orientals, the Sahibs, the Crown Imperials, the Edsels, the Vandors, the El Pollos, and above all, the Hesitations.

All but the Hesitations had a single run. The Hesitations had two. A man of faith who has recorded a gospel album, Blakey credits God for the Hesitations getting as far as they got.

There were a few missteps of his own making, and for a spell, Blakey hitched his star to an automotive failure. "I had the name before the Edsels that made 'Rama Lama Ding Dong,'" notes Blakey. "I was a car buff, and the Edsel was getting ready to come out." (Actually, Blakey's Cleveland Edsels and its homonym band from the Youngstown, Ohio suburb of Campbell worked simultaneously: Blakey was still in high school in 1957 when he sang in his group, and the other Edsels released their song in 1958. The expensive, heavy Edsel car, with its distinctive horse-collar grill, was a bomb, expiring in 1960 after just two years.)

Before he launched the Hesitations, Blakey worked with Lou Ragland and George Hendricks in the Vandors and the El Pollos. There were permutations, like a duo segment Blakey called "a Sam and Dave kind of thing" Blakey and Ragland— and, at times, Hendricks and Ragland—delivered during Vandors shows. Blakey says the Vandors were one of the first Black groups to play Cleveland's West Side, regularly working the Can Can off West 25th Street near Denison. (Dave C. and the Sharptones, featuring Black lead singer Dave Cox, also played the West Side, and was the real pioneer, Blakey says. Cox's band was largely white.)

"When we were at the Can Can, we would socialize," Blakey says, evoking a time when "people were really trying to understand each other. I'm talking about seriously melting together. People were people.

"Back in those times, the girls were the curious ones. The Black guys got next to the white girls. The difference

THAT WAS A DIFFERENT ERA. WE WERE LIKE GUNSLINGERS WITH VOICES. WE WERE FRIENDS UNTIL WE WENT ON THE STAGE

was, they found out that wasn't what I was there for. I'd bring my wife. Once they found out I was just a regular guy, my children and their children used to spend the night together."

DETROIT CALLING

THE EL POLLOS WAS a vocal group that recorded two 45s in the late '50s. The El Pollos performed their tunes "Someone to Love Me" and "One of Those Days" at the Skateland Ballroom at 9001 Euclid Avenue in late September 1958. Also on that dance card: the El Deons, Eddie Williams' doo-wop group. So much activity!

The El Pollos liked Blakey's work with the Vandors so much they asked him if he wanted to cut a record with them. Which explains Blakey's second trip to Detroit. He'd been there with the Crown Imperials, but that didn't work out well.

The El Pollos in that Motor City-bound car included future Hesitations George Scott and Robert Sheppard, along with former Metrotone Leonard Veal, another future Hesitation. So much fluidity!

Blakey, Scott and Veal were the core of the original Hesitations. They didn't want to sign with Motown, which had treated them poorly, Blakey says. "We'd all been up to Motown before, and they treated us kind of raggedy," he says. "The guys in the El Pollos had gone up and felt the same way." At one audition, Motown paid them "no attention until Mary Wells walked in and got mad with them." That early encounter with Motown poobahs soured Blakey.

I have to credit Blakey and his young buddies for persistence. They were driven enough to step out of the familiar and they wouldn't give up no matter the discouragement.

Until his first stab at Detroit, Blakey had never been out of Ohio. His only forays beyond Cleveland were to cabaret parties in places like Twinsburg and Chagrin Falls, but the prospects in Detroit lured him to cross the border.

On one trip north—Blakey thinks it was in 1965—they met a producer and arranger named Shelley Haims, who turned them on to percussionist Jack Ashford, a Funk Brother whose tambourine became a signature of Motown recordings. Haims must have liked something about the nascent Hesitations even though they failed to knock it out of the park that time, Blakey says.

At least the group impressed Haims enough for him to recommend it to Ashford, who in turn readied the Hesitations for a record deal. After Ashford molded them into a unit with commercial potential, he "turned us on to Kapp," Blakey says. Kapp was a New York record label known for Roger Williams' schmaltzy piano hits. The Hesitations made it onto the charts with gospelized vocal takes on the Williams instrumentals "Born Free" and "The Impossible Dream," in 1966 and 1967. Through an arrangement between Ashford and Gerald W. Purcell's GWP Associates, they recorded four albums for Kapp: *Soul Superman, Solid Gold, The New Born Free,* and *Where We're At!* Their peak years were 1967 and 1968. By 1969, they were largely spent.

The group didn't start its recording career auspiciously. The first time Ashford heard the Hesitations, he told them to go home and work on their harmonies. "The first time we went to do our recording, we failed because we couldn't sing together," Blakey says, sounding a familiar complaint. "We didn't have a good nucleus."

So the group returned to Cleveland, rehearsed for a full week, and refined its presentation. Several personnel changes followed before the Hesitations gave Detroit a second shot.

"All we needed was guys who knew what they were doing," Blakey says. "One person with a tin ear would disrupt the harmonies."

Their first day back in the Motor City, when Blakey, Scott and Veal hit the first note of Ashford's tune "Soul Kind of Love," everything clicked, Blakey says. "Let's make some records," Ashford said. And so they did, issuing those four albums in 1967 and 1968. They released five charting singles, too. And they got around.

Before the trip that put the Hesitations on track, Blakey had gone to Detroit with the Crown Imperials, "one of the better groups in town," but had come back empty-handed. How he returned home with a record contract for a group still in development on that second Hesitations try continues to puzzle him; he credits "the person upstairs."

In 2023 Blakey sings for the United Church of God in Grafton, Ohio. He also sings secular material with a Motown tribute band called Twist, and with the Day Nites, a gang of young virtuosos that plays original tunes.

"I've always been continuous," he says.

A COMPLICATED RIDE

TWISTS AND TURNS ALONG the way, including distribution and compensation issues, dogged the Hesitations until its first iteration expired in the early '70s after a more than respectable run and several charting singles. The last one that made any noise for the original group was issued on the GWP label. "Is This The Way To Treat A Girl (You Bet It Is)," features one of Blakey's most urgent leads.

After *Soul Superman* was released, spawning eight tracks for singles play, the group returned to the studio to record a follow-up. All might have gone smoothly but for the December 1967 death of George Scott, the group's leader. On a drive back from a wedding party, a back seat passenger passed a derringer to the front. In the transfer, the gun went off, shooting Scott in the temple. That fatal bullet badly wounded the group.

Still, on the strength of the sales of "Born Free" and "The Impossible Dream," the Hesitations recorded a concert for the Armed Forces Radio Service that paved the

way for a tour of military bases in Germany. They also performed at Harlem's iconic Apollo Theatre. Touring was one thing, however; business was another.

Despite their profile and popularity overseas, Blakey says their stateside distribution was spotty; he couldn't find Hesitations albums in record stores. And by 1969, Ashford's relationship with GWP had deteriorated, ending the deal with Kapp; the group's final singles, which Blakey says lack the plush sound of their Kapp releases, came out on GWP. When he asked GWP's Purcell to show him the books, Purcell was less than forthcoming.

Backed by the superb Day Nites, Blakey croons at a standing room only January 2023 gig at Cleveland's Beachland Ballroom.
(Photo courtesy of James O'Hare)

Blakey thinks the group was blackballed for raising such issues, suggesting that's why Kenny Gamble and Leon Huff, the owners of Philadelphia International Records, didn't sign them despite a recommendation from the O'Jays, who were stars on that label.

A SECOND WIND

DESPITE THEIR LABEL TROUBLES, the Hesitations had a track record—and, it turns out, a fan base that goes deep. Because someone in England bought out the group's contract with GWP, some vintage Hesitations material made its way onto European compact disks, generating a trickle of long-overdue royalties. The revival of old Hesitations tunes might explain why they were treated like kings at a huge Northern Soul festival in Prestatyn, UK in October 2009.

"We were there for about a week, but we didn't sing but for one day," Blakey says. "It was one of the best trips I ever had. They were very, very nice people over there." He has been getting some back royalties, "a little bit every now and then, you know? Over there, they like the old stuff more than the new stuff."

After their run at the end of the '60s and the start of the '70s, the Hesitations went silent for decades, re-emerging in 2006 in a doo-wop program at the Rock and Roll Hall of Fame. Blakey formed a new lineup with former Sahibs George Hendricks and William Carter, along with Blakey's wife, Joyce. Gig opportunities began to resurface, from the Beachland Ballroom in Cleveland to Nighttown in Cleveland Heights, even north to Erie, Pennsylvania. The band generated new material and recorded its reverent version of Luther Vandross's "Song for my Father." The Hesitations seemed on a new roll. But when Hendricks suffered a stroke in 2016, the band ground to a decisive halt.

The Hesitations were more than a contender. Only age defeated them.

"The Hesitations are gone for good, I would say," says Blakey. "I think it was one of the best times of my life; I got to do things I never thought I'd get a chance to do. I was on TV in two different countries. Before I was singing, I had never left Ohio; the furthest I'd been was Ashtabula. Singing took me to another place.

"The only thing I didn't get was the money," he says, laughing. "Did a lot of traveling but somebody else got the money."

10 *Sharp-Dressed* MAN ABOUT TOWN

GEORGE HENDRICKS LOVED SINGING ALL over Cleveland and points south. Genre didn't matter in his performances. "I sang all kinds of songs," Hendricks says, "ballads, jazz, rock. Whatever the crowd likes."

George Hendricks had so much fun in the 1960s, singing all over town, falling in and out of love, and working with the best bands. Never a band leader, Hendricks was something bigger: a star.

Hendricks gave all manner of music a smooth, easy treatment, making him a draw. Nice moves, too. "I was the ladies' man, more or less," he says.

He has special affection for Liz's Lounge, Liz Fredrickson's club on 105th Street between Euclid and Chester avenues. Liz's Lounge was smoky but cool. The stage, slightly raised from club level, was comfortable, as were the dressing rooms in the basement. "People used to come to have a good time," Hendricks says, and fans of Hendricks, a frequent vocalist for Harvey and the Phenomenals, showed up week after week. (Harvey Hall's group was a staple at Liz's Lounge into the late 1970s.)

Another factor keeping the atmosphere at Liz's chill: Cleveland police. Hendricks says Fredrickson had cultivated a friendly relationship with the men in blue from managing the nearby Esquire Lounge. The police presence made Liz's Lounge feel safe. Fredrickson was "one of my favorite people," he says. "Whenever I came into town, she'd put me to work."

Hendricks looked sharp on stage, wearing jumpsuits, a form-fitting vest, custom two-pieces (Hendricks had a black-and-white suit made for him, complete with white ruffles), many of them designed by his childhood friend Barbara White, the Phenomenals manager.

White, who lives in the same assisted living facility as Hendricks, also costumed Sweet Honesty, a group Cynthia Woodard founded. It changed its name to Ba-Roz but broke up when Woodard joined the Blossoms as a backup singer for Tom Jones.

So many connections.

Billowy shirts with big collars and vivid geometric patterns, along with polyester suits—White made them all. Hendricks was a steady customer of hers. In the '60s and '70s, fashion, like music, was free-form.

Hendricks had a big Afro for a time. And he was busy, regularly working at Liz's and, on other nights, fronting organist Sam Blackshaw's group at the Brougham Lounge across from Liz's and at the El Patio Lounge at East 138th Street and St. Clair Avenue. Also on that El Patio bill: "La danse exotique" specialist Peaches LaBanks. Born Mary Swaney, LaBanks was killed in October 1976, five weeks after her husband, Lorenzo H. Swaney, was killed at the same bar: Peaches Lounge, around 150th Street and Kinsman Avenue.

For a reporter and fan like me, there are so many rabbit holes to explore.

Hendricks was busy on the Chitlin' Circuit both inside and outside Cleveland, working in Harvey Hall's band, with the Chosen Few, and with various Lou Ragland bands.

Other places Hendricks worked include George's International Cuisine on Prospect Avenue, the Kinsman Grill on Kinsman Avenue, and the SKD Lounge on Woodhill Road. Despite all that activity, there were slow times. They got slower.

BUSY GEORGE

PICTURES OF HENDRICKS IN full 'fro, wearing a dashiki or strutting his stuff in American peacock attire show a charismatic entertainer ready, willing and able to enhance any group he played in. In bands like the Challengers, Lou Ragland's Vandors, and Joe Pearson/ Eugene Ross' Chosen Few. Even though he rarely was the leader, the limber, sexy Hendricks was the draw especially for the girls.

This persuasive vocalist drew crowds to clubs all over Cleveland's East Side and the occasional point west. Hendricks ended his performing career late

On and off stage, George Hendricks drove the girls wild.

in the Hesitations, the pop-soul band his buddy Art Blakey originally founded.

Hendricks was born in Bessemer, Alabama on August 6, 1942. He, his sister, three brothers, and their father moved to Cleveland when he was 7, following his parents' divorce. They settled in around Quincy and Central avenues, the neighborhood where Hendricks made lifelong friends of vocal peers Blakey and Ragland. Patrons of Hendricks' father's four-chair barber shop at East 79th Street and Quincy supported the family. As a kid, Hendricks had a shoe shine stand there.

Hendricks seems born to express himself. "My Mom told me that when I was 2 years old, I used to climb up on the table and try to sing," he says. As did many other Invisible Soul singers, Hendricks found his voice in church choir as a little boy.

Hendricks told cultural historian Dana Aritonovich in a 2009 clevelandvoices.org interview that seeing girls hanging around a group of boys harmonizing doo-wop convinced him the path of the vocalist would be more rewarding than the boxing career he was considering. Hendricks was probably 12 then.

He grew up with AM radio, listening to the Black station WJMO and the white station WHK, singing along with the Four Freshmen, Tony Bennett, Frank Sinatra, Johnny Mathis— and Nat "King" Cole, virtually the only Black crooner to cross over then.

Hendricks attended Quincy Elementary School, Rawlings Junior High School and John Hay High School. The 1961 John Hay graduate took guitar, voice, piano and acting lessons at Cuyahoga Community College.

In 1958, Hendricks became a founding member of the Sahibs, staying in the group until 1961.

"Every now and then, we'd have a big falling out," Hendricks recalls. "Every time one of the members of the Sahibs would leave and sing with another group they became competition." Their chief rivals were the Futuretones and the El Deons. All three groups were based in the Central-Quincy area; Blakey's Wigs and Harvey Hall's pre-Phenomenal Five Fabulous Flames were competitors, too.

Before the Sahibs, Hendricks, Blakey, Carter and Dotson were members of the Collegiates, a nine-man group

Hendricks joined on the strength of hitting an impressive high note. But the Collegiates were not stable: members got in trouble with the law, Blakey was in a car accident, and some left to join the Crown Imperials, the precursor to Alphonso Boyd's Imperial Wonders.

The Sahibs, with Hendricks and Blakey as its nucleus, made its debut at a talent show at John Hay. They began presenting more and more shows, publicized by WJMO general manager (and Hendricks champion) Ken Hawkins. "We would go to hospitals and schools. We did a lot of charity work, we never got paid." Hendricks says. "We just loved singing, we got the exposure, and Ken Hawkins was the man at the time."

Hendricks, particularly in his early days, walked a teetering line between wildness and responsibility. His career spans performance, recording, business—and propagation. He often found himself between groups and between women.

"My biggest problem has always been being impatient," he says. "I got more patience now than when I was younger." As much a ladies' man as a family man, Hendricks has 13 children, not all of them with his four wives.

This man-about-town also worked in the Vandors, an early Ragland band featuring three guitarists and the explosive drummer "Wild Bill" Matlock, and later Ragland bands like the Bandmasters. Ultimately, however, family life won over nightlife. But the picture was never totally black and white, whether on the professional level or the personal level. As best he could, Hendricks lived and worked in several worlds.

BRIDGING THE GAP

DURING THE '60S AND early '70s, Cleveland was "very separated," Hendricks says: The West Side was 90-percent white, the East Side 90-percent Black, but sometimes the twain met. When the Vandors played the Can Can on West 25th Street, club management "would actually tell us we were allowed to perform but not mingle out in the audience too much," Hendricks recalls. The obvious reason was racism:

"They didn't want you around the girls." That was also true in other clubs, particularly on the West Side, but as Blacks started moving there and integrating with the area's school systems, things began to change.

"It's still not that easy (for a Black band) to get into an all-white club unless you had a white manager and at least two white members," Hendricks says, though having a woman in the group "seems to take away from the fear: If you saw five Black guys back in those days, there'd be some tension, but it seemed to relax a bit if there was a female involved."

In 1964, Hendricks was drafted into the Army, forcing him to quit the Bandmasters, a Ragland group that succeeded the Vandors and also backed up the vocalist and style queen Kim Tolliver. On his way into the military, Hendricks also sang in the Challengers, a rhythm and blues group featuring his childhood friend Ann Bogan. Before the Army, Hendricks was busy both on stage and in the studio. Not only did he wax unreleased material at Boddie Recording, Hendricks vocals that actually surfaced include backup on the Rojac single "Let Them Talk/I'll Try To Do Better" with Cleveland soul diva Tolliver ("another Tina Turner"), and lead vocal on "Love Power/Barbara," a Red Top and the Young Family 45 released on Tri-City, a Saginaw, Michigan label. As part of the Challengers, he recorded for Tri-Phi, a pre-Motown label Harvey Fuqua of Moonglows fame launched in 1961. (In the late '50s, when Hendricks was still a student at Rawlings Junior High, the Moonglows used to rehearse in a place on Lucia Avenue off East 79th Street between Central and Quincy avenues. Marvin Gaye was the Moonglows drummer then.)

Hendricks actually traveled to the soul-music Mecca of Muscle Shoals, Alabama with Tolliver twice, backing her on *Let Them Talk*, an album on Rojac Records. The record was produced by her husband, Freddie Briggs, and featured Stax studio musicians who had backed Isaac Hayes, the deep-voiced singer famous for the theme music from the movie Shaft. Label owner Jack Taylor also was Hendricks' manager for a time in the early 1970s.

Hendricks thinks Tolliver should have hit. She certainly made a local splash. She also grazed the big time recording *Come and Get Me—I'm Ready*, a polished rhythm and blues album for Chess, a Chicago label known for its recordings of Howlin' Wolf, Muddy Waters, and Chuck Berry.

"She was known basically for soulful singing and her wardrobe," Hendricks says. "She used to dress like crazy. She designed all her own gowns and was said to change clothes every time she sang a song.

"She was very spiritual, too, and started off singing in church, which most of us did. Kim was, like, the entertainers' mother. Kim used to cook for everybody. You could come to her house at 3 or 4 in the morning and if there were any entertainers in town, they would be over there eating."

Hendricks also recorded two tunes written by Briggs at Golden World, Don Davis's Detroit studio, adding piano parts at Boddie., but they, too, remain unreleased.

PATRIOT GEORGE

HENDRICKS SPENT A TOTAL of four years in the Army. He first served at Fort Gordon in Augusta, Georgia, returning to Cleveland in 1966 for a year at the Nike base in Bratenahl. He then reenlisted for another two years—in Vietnam.

The July 15, 1967 issue of the *Call & Post*, Cleveland's Black newspaper, covers a going-away party at the Gay Cossack Lounge on Union Avenue for "singer-soldier" Hendricks. "Before he went into the service, Hendricks had sung with the Sahibs, a popular Cleveland group, and with the Challengers who recorded 'Honey, Honey, Honey,'" the weekly notes.

Girls love a man in uniform.

"Stationed with the 90th Artillery Battery in Warrensville Heights, Hendricks soldiered during the week and became

> **I REMEMBER GIRLS COMING TO THE SHOWS WITH THEIR CASSETTE RECORDERS AND POLAROID CAMERAS.**

'The Swinging Soldier Singer' on weekends, mostly at the Gay Cossack." The paper says artists from Way Out Recording and Boddie would be Hendricks's "special guests" that weekend and the next. Hendricks was in the thick of Black Cleveland's musical scene. Don Carter, the *Call & Post's* sales director, frequently mentioned Hendricks in his Happenings column.

"The last gig I had before going to Vietnam was at Gleason's Show Bar," Hendricks told clevelandvoices.org. "If you made it to Gleason's you hit the big time. That's where all the entertainers went in those days. The Beatles were popular at that time; we had a skit about the Beatles and wore Beatle wigs, and we would come in singing 'She Loves You' as the Black Beatles (not to be confused with the Wigs, the faux British Invasion band Blakey headed).

"We didn't have a Motown mentality in Cleveland; if there was, there would be a lot more visual history. I remember girls coming to the shows with their cassette recorders and recording the shows; they had Polaroids then." That gig was in spring 1964. According to the *Call & Post*, "Jap" Gleason sold his club to Gloria Lawrence and Al Howell that September. They remodeled, installed a dance floor, and reopened as the House of Blues.

What happened to those Polaroids is anybody's guess.

IN THE TRADITION

WHEN HENDRICKS ENTERED THE field, entertainment was all over the map.

"We had revues, maybe four or five acts on the show, and any of those shows could have gone to Vegas and done great," he says. "Normally, we used to have a show band and they played for everybody. You would normally have an MC/comedian like Charles Eckstein, Sad Sam and Eli- Tel-A-Lie, and male dancers. Sometimes we had four or five dancers." Of various genders.

Billed as exotic dancers, burlesque queens entered a room fully gowned but ended stripped down to a G string. Show bands like the Fabulations titillated patrons of Robert's Steak House and Party Center, an after-hours BYOB at 140th Street and Kinsman Road, and Don Gregory & the Montclairs was the house band at the Music Box at 106th Street and Euclid and, for a time, Don King's Corner Tavern. The Bandmasters—which Ragland formed in the early '70s—rotated between the Music Box and Gleason's when they weren't on the road with Tolliver. Wednesday night was "Happy Feet Night" at the Music Box; that's also the name of a Gregory/Montclairs instrumental that became a regional smash. It was produced by Carl Maduri, the Cleveland record-industry pioneer who went on to produce Wild Cherry's "Play That Funky Music."

Hendricks also sang male lead—and absorbed a lot about show business—in Ubiquity 12, a troupe of mixed gender, most of them dancers. "Talk about professionals," he says. "I learned a lot about entertainment, being on shows with them."

If it feels like Hendricks' reminiscences are run-on, that's because his life felt non-stop: Going to 105 was "like being in Times Square," he says.

Hendricks' eyes shine brighter when he thinks of the many places that are gone. The Alhambra, which used to be a bowling alley, was located on East 102nd Street and

As solo acts and especially when teamed up, George Hendricks (at left) and his old friend Lou Ragland were a soulful force.

Euclid Avenue, an intersection that no longer exists—at Euclid. Beneath the Alhambra was the Red Carpet Lounge, a nightclub with entertainment. Across the street, now occupied by the Clinic (as is the whole area), was Club 100, a jazz club. Farther west, the Road South, a show bar, presented local and national acts including the Imperial Wonders and the Bar-Kays.

"I used to sing at Liz's Lounge on 105, leave after the first show, go to the Continental way on the other side of town, leave there and go to the Round Table," Hendricks says.

The Continental wasn't that far away, around 127th and St. Clair near Shaw; the Round Table at 83rd and Quincy.

Hendricks was a natural—and a sucker—for the stage, even one in a combat zone.

He doesn't remember the name of the soul band he led in Vietnam, only that it included guitar, bass, sax, drums, with him on vocals; they went into jungle the USO couldn't reach, playing "anything that was popular to remind the guys of home." Two captains looking for a vocalist pressed Hendricks into that unusual gig.

Hendricks' job in Vietnam was putting up telephone lines and poles. He escaped injury. "I was blessed," he says. "I saw guys next to me get shot. I've seen guys blown up."

When he returned home from Vietnam, Hendricks plunged back into Cleveland's vibrant soul scene, hooking up with Ragland in the Vandors. They rehearsed at Ragland's house at East 88th Street and Hough Avenue. "We were young and wild and the girls loved us," Hendricks says, laughing. "We thought we were almost there, that was it."

The civil rights movement was mature when Hendricks returned to the United States in 1968. Martin Luther King Jr. and Robert F. Kennedy had been assassinated, and the riots in Hough and Glenville continued to scar Cleveland; still, though the country was by no means free of prejudice, it felt better to him, if far from peaceful.

Upon his return, Hendricks ran into love trouble: a woman he was dating got miffed when she came across pictures of him with Vietnamese women, so Hendricks got busy back on the circuit. He resumed his singing career as lead vocalist with Harvey and the Phenomenals, and worked in a trio with a drummer named Connie and sometime saxophonist Fred "Ahmed" Evans. (Evans, who was convicted of murder in fatally shooting four people in the 1968 Glenville Shootout, died of cancer in 1978 at age 46.) Hendricks, who returned to a Cleveland patrolled by the National Guard, bought a gun for self-defense and accidentally nearly shot his buddy Ragland at the Liberty Theater at 103rd and Superior that Ragland and Way Out Records executive Billy Branch owned.

In October 1977, the *Call & Post* predicted that Hendricks, along with "recording star" Ragland as co-leader of the "mighty" Chosen Few Band, would "proceed to tear the roof off the atmospheric 'Blue Room' with every performance."

Wish I'd been at the SKD Lounge on Woodhill Road there to see these veteran soulmen raise that roof.

WINDING DOWN

BY THE EARLY '70S, Hendricks had been a professional musician all his

Hendricks (to Blakey's right) and a group of Invisible Soul-era luminaries gather at Blakey's performance in March 2023.

life. Family demands moved him onto a more regular, more reliable track.

Until a stroke ended his entertainment career—and the revival of the Hesitations, his last group—Hendricks worked. Until the '70s, work was night-time. After that, day jobs came to dominate.

His profession as a vocalist conflicted with his family responsibilities. At the same time, performing gave him space away from his teeming domestic situation.

"All that was good when it was just me," Hendricks says, looking back fondly on more than 50 years as a full-time entertainer. But by the time he had five children to support, he needed steady and secure income. He briefly worked for United Parcel Service, was a supervisor for Dairy Mart, and owned the Inner-City Beverage Store at 82nd and Superior. He also managed and co-owned Lady J's, a bar at 18th Street and Carnegie, which he eventually sold to Cleveland State.

Hendricks also worked at American Steel & Wire Co. for 13 years, ending in 2001. He put a lid on his business career as a regional manager for a janitorial company doing maintenance for Home Depots in Northeast Ohio around the time the Hesitations started a fresh battle for the spotlight.

"I was singing all the time," he says.

His last show-business act was with the Hesitations. That band ground to a halt when a stroke kneecapped Hendricks in January 2016.

"Music was entertaining to other people," says this affable and charming man, "and it was entertaining to me. Music has made me, I would say, a popular person in spiritual music and rock and roll."

Bridges

- Genre irrelevant
- Able to cross
  east o west

Borders

- Modern
- Rare

division

11 BIG WHEEL *on* a *Bumpy Road*

Lou Ragland did it all: sing, write, arrange, produce, lead bands—and that's just the music part. Ragland was much more than a contender. He should have been a smash.

LOU RAGLAND WAS A NATURAL MUSICIAN, a handyman, a landlord, a theater owner, a window washer, a marketer. He was smart with a buck, improvisational, and as disciplined as he was creative. His high tenor was sweet solo, velvet in harmony. Were it not for fickle luck, the vagaries of the music business, and, perhaps, spreading himself too thin, this groove master would have been a far greater commercial success.

No matter: His 60-year career covered doo-wop, soul, funk and pop, all with his own twist. A versatile original, he was far more than a contender. Lou Ragland was an Invisible Soul face.

Louis Edward Ragland cut his teeth in Cleveland lounges, from the Brougham to the Mayflower Gold to Trina's to the Gay Cossack. His venues spanned high-school competitions, clubs on both sides of the city, and theaters on the Chitlin' Circuit. His complicated, restless story begs for a full biography. Ragland offered me that opportunity in 2020, but it was too late. He died of cancer that August 19, leaving behind his wife Stella and eight children.

Ragland and I bonded in 2013, when the Rock and Roll Hall of Fame set up a conversation between us as part of the museum's Black History Month celebration. I had interviewed Ragland by phone a few times but had never met him in person, and I sensed a wariness in him, a reluctance to be open to someone he didn't know, yet another white guy eager to plunder him for exclusive information without offering anything in return.

Years after the event, while rooting around my archives, I rediscovered how the Rock Hall billed us:

Wednesday, February 13 at 7pm

An Evening with Lou Ragland

Rock and Roll Hall of Fame and Museum's Foster Theater

Born on the east side of Cleveland, Ohio in 1942, Lou Ragland has donned many hats in his long career. He's a singer, guitarist, songwriter, record producer, studio engineer, and more. Ragland's first 45, "Never Let Me Go/Party at Lester's," was recorded in 1960 at Boddie Recording Studio on Union Avenue and released on the Way Out label the following year.

Between the late 1960s and mid-1970s, Ragland produced some of Cleveland's greatest soul music, leading such groups as Hot Chocolate, Volcanic Eruption and Seven Miles High. In 1977, he released the solo album, The ConVeyor, on his own SMH label.

Besides recording for local labels, Ragland also recorded singles for Amy and Warner Brothers. Before he became the O'Jays road manager in 1967, he was the only African American in the Terry Knight Revue, playing guitar alongside Cleveland saxophone legend Ernie Krivda. Knight went on to manage Grand Funk Railroad. Ragland will be interviewed by Carlo Wolff, author of *Cleveland Rock & Roll Memories.*

I marinated in anxiety for a few days, girding myself by creating a single-spaced list of topics and questions that spilled onto a second page. I brought it to the table Ragland and I shared on the stage of the Rock Hall's intimate theater, a perfect setting for a talk. After we were introduced, I started on the list. Ragland seemed instantly at ease answering questions about his singular career.

About two minutes in, I laid down the list —and conversation flowed freely for nearly 75 minutes. Not only was the audience mesmerized, some members had questions, and many of them were eager to talk after the event. It felt like yet another homecoming for Ragland, who had returned to Cleveland the previous August for a Hot Chocolate reunion at the Beachland Ballroom. Ragland made, marketed and performed music from the late 1950s until his death at 78.

A native of Cleveland's Central area, Ragland grew up in a creative family: his brother is an artist, his sister a dancer, and early on, he showed musical talent, taking up the saxophone at age 12. He also played tuba, drums and clarinet, guitar, and bass. Music was his destiny.

"Lou has been actively plodding (cq) toward a career as a song stylist since school days at East High School and at one time headed a group of singers known as the Sahibs," the *Call & Post* reported on March 30, 1965. "Now defunct, the Sahibs enjoyed a great deal of local popularity while singing before teen dances and cabaret parties. Unfortunately, draft notices and tonsillectomies eventually caused the group to break up." The article notes that despite that setback, Ragland persevered, working days at a manufacturing plant and playing engagements at night. His weekend gig, Cleveland's Black newspaper said, was at West Brook's Lounge on the city's West Side, a part of Cleveland where few Black entertainers ventured.

A TASTE OF NATIONWIDE

IN A JULY 30, 1965 follow-up about Ragland, the *Call & Post* claimed that the original March 30 article about the promising and industrious musician, written by *C&P* reporter Effie M. Burrus, led Billy Ward, leader of the Dominoes, to call Ragland, asking him whether he'd be interested in becoming the lead singer of Ward's rhythm and blues group.

"In 1965, I was a solo artist with my very own band, Lou Ragland and the Band Masters," Ragland told r&b historian Marv Goldberg in the October 1995 issue of the record collector magazine *Discoveries*. He noted that his first single was "Never Let Me Go"/"Party At Lester's," cut at Cleveland Recording for Way Out Records, the Cleveland label owned by former Hornets singer Lester Johnson, William "Little Mama Red" Thompson, and Bill Branch.

His partners "wrote numbers, played numbers," Branch said. "This is what their lives were about, but the record company was over and above that. It was a labor of love. They loved music, they loved entertainers." Branch noted that Don King, the numbers and boxing kingpin who became publisher of the *Call & Post*, approached Way Out as a possible investor, but "we couldn't work it out." Branch said there was a strict separation between the owners' private lives and the company, and between his work as a cop and whatever activities his partners were involved in. Like the numbers, music was a game of chance.

Cleveland Browns greats Jim Brown and Walter Roberts later became part-owners of Way Out. Ragland's Bandmasters supplied the instrumentals for Ragland's single. The Sahibs served up background vocals.

That summer, Ragland was performing at the Music Box in Cleveland's Central area when one of the club's owners heard that Ward was reorganizing the Dominoes and sent Ward Ragland's 45 and photo. Ward sent Ragland a train ticket; Ragland wouldn't fly. At 23, helming the Dominoes, a group with a national fan base looked like a ticket to the big time (not to mention the honor of filling the shoes of r&b greats Clyde McPhatter and Jackie Wilson).

Ragland arrived in Los Angeles on August 11, the first day of the Watts Riots, moving into a small apartment on Hollywood Boulevard above a Fred Astaire dance studio. Ward, who lived in a suite on the floor above, had already laid down instrumental tracks for an upcoming Dominoes album. Ragland was to sing lead; for backup, he recommended Cleveland buddy Benny Butcher, a sometime Sahib. Ward flew Butcher out. Ragland recorded four tracks.

He spent about four months with Ward, returning home after Ward refused to credit him as lead on those tunes. He got home on his own; he'd held onto the $500 he brought with him to Los Angeles. Ward had paid Ragland $400 a week—before charging him $300 for room and board.

"I drove Billy Ward's new lady friend's car back to Sloan, Iowa and took a train home from there," Ragland told Goldberg. "After I was home for just 12 hours, Billy Ward flew in to talk to my mother. He asked her to persuade me to return to the group, but we had the same problem with the label credit. As far as I know the Dominoes ended then, but the records got released." (Ragland's vocals were erased and recorded over—and the Dominoes soldiered on for a few years.)

BANDMASTER LOU

BACK HOME, RAGLAND RESUMED work at Way Out. "I was the first artist they produced on Way Out, and after they found out that I could engineer and play instruments they didn't do any more on me," Ragland said, explaining his stint there. "They didn't want to lose me to the art world, they wanted me to pump out these songs."

Ragland quickly became a player in Cleveland's soul scene as a producer at local labels Way Out and Saru and as a bass player with the O'Jays and later as their road manager. In 1969, after George Hendricks returned from Vietnam, Ragland rejoined his lifelong friend in the Sahibs.

During the '60s and '70s, Ragland also played in a gang of other bands including Hot Chocolate, Seven Miles High, the Vandors, Volcanic Eruption, and The Chosen Few. "I started every group I named except for the Sahibs," he said. "My first group was the Bandmasters. I was in the Sahibs in 1959 and 1960." He and Hendricks launched Volcanic Eruption in 1967, but Hendricks went back into the service in Vietnam that same year. James McLain of the Springers replaced him; the group sputtered on until 1968, when Ragland joined the O'Jays organization as road manager. By that time, he knew his way around a studio, capitalizing on skills he learned at Way Out. He also learned production at Don White's Agency Recording Studios above the Agora on East 24th Street. Ragland recorded a song called "Traveling Man" for Way Out at Cleveland Recording. He recorded two more tunes there in July 1975. So did his band Volcanic Eruption.

TRYING TIMES

ALL THIS MUSICAL ACTIVITY was taking place against a wildly unstable backdrop. The 1960s were famously volatile, even dangerous. The Hough Riots drew the National Guard to Cleveland in July 1966, and almost exactly two years later, the Glenville Shootout deepened the scars on a large swath of Cleveland's East Side.

Memories of a competition at the Circle Ballroom on 105 between Art Blakey's Collegiates and the Sahibs prompted Blakey to recall a horrific incident involving Ragland on July 18, 1966, the day the Hough Riots ignited—and Ragland's 24th birthday. Ragland lived on East 88th Street in the Hough neighborhood.

"The night of the Hough Riots we were at Lou Ragland's birthday party," said Blakey. "That night Ragland's girlfriend was killed."

Authorities blamed the convulsion on snipers, Blakey said, adding Ragland's girlfriend was the first person killed in the five days of pillage, arson and bloodshed. The riots disfigured the Hough neighborhood on Cleveland's East Side, effectively extinguishing a vibrant, walkable entertainment district.

As the turbulence spread, police were getting people off the street, including Ragland's girlfriend. "They told us she went upstairs in the apartment but she didn't know where some of her children were and she went to the window yelling, My kid, my kid, my kid, and the police yelled, Get back in; she's yelling for her kid, we got people shooting at the police, police shot at the window and killed Joyce," said Blakey. They shot her by mistake, he said: "We had a chaotic state and they were trying to get order… the way the police knew she was shot was people brought her body down the steps."

In the *Plain Dealer* of July 19, 1966, a Leon McCord said he was walking with his wife and Joyce Arnett on East 73rd Street when "they came upon a group of policemen trying to contain what McCord said was a mob." Cops pushed the three into an apartment building "out of the way of gunfire." But Arnett became hysterical, and stuck her head out of the window, shouting, 'I want to go home. My God, I want to go home to my kids.'" At that point, the mother of three was hit with a bullet in the right side of her head. She was pronounced dead at Mount Sinai Hospital. (Thanks to James Robenalt for steering me to source material.)

Misfortune wasn't Ragland's normal environment, however.

A rare agency promo shot of Ragland (courtesy of Abdul Ghani)

EXTENDING A HAND

ON AND OFF STAGE, Ragland was bold. Ragland was anything but risk-averse. He took chances on people and was willing to try on different styles and approaches. He also knew how to engender loyalty.

It was pouring rain. Eugene Ross, a multi-instrumentalist, vocalist and artist, was driving past Juva' De, a nightclub on Harvard Avenue, when he saw a man moving equipment.

He glanced at the marquee, saw it featured Lou Ragland and The Chosen Few, turned around, and pulled into the club's driveway.

After they introduced themselves, Ragland asked Ross whether he was in the music business. Ross told Ragland he'd been playing guitar for about a year, adding he was a fan of Ragland's records. "Where's the rest of the band?" Ross asked. They'd taken off, Ragland said.

Ross sensed an opportunity to help a star like Ragland as well as his own fortunes. In short order, the two loaded out the gear, then Ragland invited Ross to his Hough apartment to rehearse and see if he was a fit to join The Chosen Few. Ross wasn't so sure. "I don't think I'm good enough," he said. You never know till you try, Ragland told him. So Ross took a chance on the informal tryout, and Ragland took a chance and hired Ross. Another impromptu scenario, contribution, and collaboration, playing out during Cleveland's Invisible Soul era. "He said you never know till you try."

Ragland took a chance and hired Ross. "I think I was better than I gave myself credit for, because I have a good ear," says Ross. That version of The Chosen Few lasted until 1980, when Ragland left for Las Vegas and the ubiquitous George Hendricks took his place. (Ross said he and Hendricks were Cub Scouts together. Ross's sister Gloria occasionally sang with Ragland's group Hot Chocolate. Ross's full-time gig was sales rep for the *Cleveland Press*; he was the 's first Black to hold that position in the long-defunct afternoon newspaper.)

TAKING CARE OF BUSINESS

RAGLAND WAS NO STRANGER to hustle. Before he joined the O'Jays in a business capacity, taking over

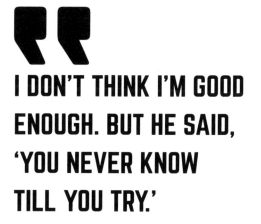

I DON'T THINK I'M GOOD ENOUGH. BUT HE SAID, 'YOU NEVER KNOW TILL YOU TRY.'

management from Leo's Casino owners Jules Berger and Leo Frank, he made money all kinds of ways: as a window washer servicing those tall buildings in Shaker Heights, converting furnaces from coal to gas, even profiting off recycling. He also became known for his instrumental versatility, playing guitar and bass and a guitar synthesizer he dubbed the guitorgan.

"Finally, the O'Jays made me into their business person," he recalled, noting that 1968 was the first year he "started making money from the recording business." Recruited by Bobby Massey, the group's second tenor and baritone, Ragland began his association with the highly popular group as a sideman in their touring band. "They hired me as a bass player for three weeks and during that three weeks I had to sleep in my car with a pocketful of money and I didn't like that," Ragland said. On a drive home from a Boston date, he asked the group why they weren't staying in a hotel instead of sleeping in their car. The band blamed Berger and Frank's Prime Management—and Ragland took over. The job also required marketing, a skill Ragland developed at Way Out, where he designed promotional material.

"I started with them as a seller of their pictures at every show, and I'd give them a cut of the money. I'd give them a bigger cut if they autographed the pictures," he said. He also spread his musical wings, stepping in as bassist when David Johnson quit. "Bobby Massey knew I played the guitar and knew I was friends with (O'Jays guitarist) Russell Evans— and we had about 10 days before they opened up their first gig," Ragland said. Massey bought Ragland a bass and an amplifier and Evans taught him O'Jays songs. "I brought him into the game," said Massey. "I needed a bass player and he was a guitar player."

In the late '60s, Ragland also took on the role of impresario, allying with Way Out co-owner Bill Branch and other investors in the Liberty Theater on the north side of Superior Road just east of East 105th Street. Ragland's soulmate Hendricks was one of several local greats to perform there in 1968.

CROSSTOWN TRAFFIC

IN THE LATE 1960s, Ragland also played guitar in the Terry Knight Revue, the immediate successor to Terry Knight and the Pack, the group Knight headed before forming the wildly successful rock band Grand Funk Railroad. Ragland was the only Black in the Revue; other members included saxophonists Ernie Krivda and Bob Kubec, bassist Tom Baker, and drummer Val Kent. Baker, a noted producer, arranger and multi-instrumentalist, recruited Ragland. Ragland said Knight stiffed them on pay. (Knight's daughter's boyfriend stabbed Knight to death in November 2004. That's a macabre story in itself.)

Krivda and Kent also played in the Tom Baker Quintet, a jazz combo featuring Baker on trumpet. Baker's group had a steady weekend gig at the English Grille at 105th and Euclid. At the scene's peak, there were 13 clubs within a two-to-three-mile radius some might have called Sin City. It was also a red-light district, Krivda noted.

According to Baker, the Terry Knight Revue didn't record under its own name but may have recorded as Terry Knight, releasing "Lullaby/Such a Lonely Life" as a single on Capitol. Musicians playing on that "could have been Val and me and Lou," said Baker, who arranged the tune piccolo, strings and all. "It's a totally white production," Baker added. "Don't ask me what I mean by white." Baker said he thinks it was recorded at Ken Hamann's Cleveland Recording, where Grand Funk Railroad, far and away Knight's most successful vehicle, also recorded.

Knight hired Baker as his music director; around the same time, Baker became music director of *Upbeat*, Herman Spero's musical variety show.

In the mid-60s, Baker and his buddies caught a lot of Motown acts at Leo's, including ones backed by the Funk Brothers, Motown's famous house band. There was no official house band per se at Leo's. If the act was local, like the O'Jays, the backup band would "be guys from Way Out Records," Baker said, "but when we played there it was all the primary acts at Motown." If the Motown act was major, like the Four Tops or the Supremes, Berry Gordy's organization would import the Funk Brothers from Detroit and "they would contract me to get all the additional instruments, like horns and strings, whatever they needed for arrangements. But if it was someone not that big, like Martha and the Vandellas, they would contract me to get all the players."

Traffic between Cleveland and Detroit was heavy for musicians in the late '60s and early '70s. Baker recalled an encounter involving the well-connected Ragland and David Ruffin, the beanpole lead singer of the Temptations, who went on to a solo career before his death by accidental cocaine overdose in 1991. Ruffin was 50.

"Lou Ragland knew all those Motown guys," Baker said. "How he knew them I'm not sure. When we went to Detroit one time, he said to me, We're going over to David Ruffin's house. So we went over to David Ruffin's house and Lou Ragland and I sat in David Ruffin's living room." What did you do there? "Just hang. Lou Ragland knew him somehow; there was no way somebody off the street would be able to get in his house. I think we probably smoked dope, something like that."

At Way Out, Ragland played on sessions for various groups. He also cut "I Travel Alone/Big Wheel," tunes he wrote with Baker, a key label producer. They landed on Amy, a national label, but didn't chart in the United States. Like other Ragland tunes, they became popular in England, where Northern Soul flourishes.

At the start of the 1970s, Ragland formed his longest-lived group.

TOO MUCH CHOCOLATE

HOT CHOCOLATE WAS A band Ragland put together that achieved some Chitlin' Circuit fame in the early 1970s, but Ragland's band isn't the one people think of when the name comes up. If it rings bells at all, it's likely because a British group with that handle released "You Sexy Thing," a mid-70s hit. Here's how Ragland told that story to me in 2012.

Initially recorded at Cleveland Recording, and recorded again at Agency Recording, Hot Chocolate found its commercial footing with a third recording, this time at Tom and Louise Boddie's shellac factory on Union Avenue. Ragland played guitar and organ, George Pickett bass, and Tony Roberson drums. *I Travel Alone*, a three-CD/four-LP Ragland box set Numero Group released in 2012, is worth getting for the many Hot Chocolate tracks alone.

Funksters at their peak

The group pressed 1,000 copies of its eponymous and only album, garnering airplay for "Good for the Gander," a throbbing slice of funk as irresistible as anything from Sly and the Family Stone. Airplay? Not on the album, only on the "Gander" 45, Ragland recalled. He accused Terry Knight, that controversial record figure from Flint, Michigan, of giving the Hot Chocolate name to the English group "because he didn't think they were ever going to come here … we were named Hot Chocolate in 1970, and they came out in 1973." Ragland also recalled "some kind of legislation where we stopped them in New York, and there was a payoff, and we changed our name to Seven Miles High."

When the British group landed in New York, Gerald Kushnick, a lawyer Ragland's group had hired, along with help from the musicians' union, froze the visitors'

bank accounts. Ultimately, Ragland relinquished the Hot Chocolate name in a settlement that also affected former Sly and the Family Stone bassist Larry Graham, who had agreed to produce a band named—you guessed it—Hot Chocolate. Ultimately, Graham formed a band called Graham Central Station.

"Ours was the first Hot Chocolate, in 1970,"said Ragland. "We were a hot commodity in Cleveland and all the way down the East Coast. Before the Commodores were big— they were still in school in Birmingham, Alabama—they were our opening act." (The Commodores, who recorded for the Motown label, hit with ballads like "Easy" and "Three Times a Lady," also packing clubs with funk indelibles like "Brick House" and "I Feel Sanctified." Lionel Richie was a Commodore.)

In 1971, Hot Chocolate assumed its most commercial form in an album, Ragland's first.

"We had practiced enough," he recalled."We had about 30 songs and narrowed them down to those that the people requested, so we just sat down in the studio and created one of our sets over again, and when we found out that 'Good for the Gander' was one of the best songs, we recorded that."

Hot Chocolate performed everywhere, from Pensacola to Montreal. "Almost every state in between, everything east of the Mississippi we probably covered. The Chitlin' Circuit, as they called it."

What might have been Ragland's closest—but also most insulting—brush with fame was "Since You Said You'd Be Mine," an extravagant pop-soul track he fashioned featuring layers of Hot Chocolate instrumentals along with horns, strings and background vocals. When Agency Recording engineer Arnie Rosenberg played it for Carl Maduri,

a music business legend who worked with numerous labels as singer, producer and promoter, Maduri sent the track to Warner Brothers. That label doctored it to Ragland's displeasure, production was credited to Maduri, and Hot Chocolate got no credit at all. In addition, the B side contained a typo on the label, Ragland said. Maduri and Ragland each had half of the publishing.

"We didn't have a great relationship through the years," Maduri said, indicating the single wasn't properly promoted and Ragland might have felt stiffed on royalties. "In those days, everybody complained how much the royalties were, you know?" But, he added, "it's still getting played."

NO HONOR AT HOME

BY THE MID-70s, WHILE entrenched in the music business, Ragland felt like a prophet without honor in his hometown.

"Over the past few months Ragland has appeared with his group, Seven Miles High, in clubs and on stages from New York City to Mobile, Ala.," Michael Ward reported in the May 30, 1975 *Plain Dealer*. "Last year his recording of 'Since You Said You'd Be Mine' was among the top 75 most successful soul records in the United Kingdom.

Ragland's Ink Spots

"Everywhere, it seems, doors open for Ragland. Everywhere, that is except Cleveland, the town where he was born on July 18, 1942—and the place he still calls home."

As he prepared for an all-Ohio tour, Ragland told the paper his driving ambition was local recognition. "We would love to appear at the Front Row," said Ragland, referencing a theater-in-the-round in Highland Heights that went out of business in 1993. He called himself a "pioneer" of pop-soul.

Toward the end of the '70s, Ragland commandeered several groups and continued to produce, compose and tour. He also poured his creativity into a massive solo project: *The ConVeyor*, the crowning achievement of his Cleveland career. Where the original Hot Chocolate was a testament to compactness, the smoking issue of a power trio with a funk supercharger who stuffed themselves into Ragland's '65 Mustang to dash from gig to gig, *The ConVeyor* is a lush, widescreen testament presenting Ragland as a kind of medium who used music to inspire social and spiritual change.

Released on his own label SMH, the album is ambitious and powerful. It evokes Marvin Gaye, the Temptations, and Sam Cooke, but is very much its own animal. And by featuring all kinds of local talent, from future Dazz Band trumpeter Pierre DeMudd to trombonist Fred Wheatt (a Leo's house band regular) to Bell Telefunk conga man Carlos Martinez and future O'Jays keyboardist Dunn Pearson Jr., Ragland essentially wrapped a bow on his Cleveland career.

Subtitled "He says 'Understand Each Other,'" the album "contains no artificial or mechanical substances but is a reflection of natural and pure vibrations." The cover shows Ragland flanked by a saber-toothed tiger and a dove, a "conveyor" of harmony and understanding. The back features Arabic writing and credits everyone involved.

The politically savvy entertainer said the SMH acronym stands for spiritual motion and harmony, and he appointed Fannie Lewis, who would become a memorable Cleveland City Council representative for Hough, its president for a year. "I was in business with my mother and Fannie and a couple of other ladies," Ragland said. "They were all part of my board."

According to the exceptionally well-researched liner notes for *I Travel* Alone, the Numero Group's Ragland anthology, Ragland in 1977 began to regard the Muslim Lateef Mahmud "as his spiritual guru in a brief flirtation with Islam," and Mahmud gets a producer credit on *The ConVeyor*. Numero suggests that Ragland's "dance with Islam" alienated his band mates, prompting Seven Miles High to leave their founder and record on their own in Chicago. Ragland walking off stage because his religion barred music making was one of the last straws.

Besides *The ConVeyor*, Ragland rerecorded "Tend To Your Business," a track from the album, as a single by Wildfire. "The first thing I did on SMH Records was to record the album," Ragland said. "Then I pulled the single off, 'What Can I Do/Understand Each other,' and re-recorded it. Then I recorded the group Wildfire. I sang in both groups while I was in Seven Miles High," maybe three years after Hot Chocolate.

As Hot Chocolate waned, so did Ragland's affection for Cleveland.

After his parents died, Ragland left Cleveland for good in 1980, traveling to Los Angeles and living off part-time social services work and proceeds from sales of *The ConVeyor* out of his car trunk. In 1981, after another piecemeal year, Ragland went to Las Vegas, forming the Great Lakes Orchestra and the record company Great Lakes Records. He continued making music to the end, both online and live. His last Cleveland gigs were a remarkable Hot Chocolate reunion concert in Cleveland at the Beachland Ballroom in January 2012 and a rousing gathering of old associates at a University Settlement benefit in Slavic Village in May 2018. (Full disclosure: I helped arrange that Homecoming Dance show by Lou Ragland and his All-Star Revue.)

Ragland ended his remarkable performing career in the Ink Spots, proud heirs of a legendary vocal group dating back to the 1930s. According to the Ragland obituary in the August 23, 2020 *Las Vegas Review-Journal*, he became a member of the act in 1978 and its front man in 1993. He said he owned the name the World Famous Ink Spots.

It is ironic that Ragland, who placed such high value on originality—and fought for it on behalf of his own work—took shelter in perpetuating the work of a legacy group like the Ink Spots, which disbanded in 1954.

Ragland's solo single, "I Travel Alone," was popular among R&B fans in the U.K. The record was made possible by fellow Cleveland artist and friend Edwin Starr, who connected Ragland to Bell Records," *Review-Journal* columnist John Katsilometes wrote. (Bell was a subsidiary of Amy.)

Numero Group and the British label Soul Brother, which reissued *The ConVeyor*, are the only companies that paid him in all the time he was recording, Ragland told me in November 2011. "The folks over in England, those guys over there, paid me quite a bit of money, royalties and statements, so I have the utmost respect for those guys." Respect and support long overdue such a singular and funky talent.

ACID ACCUSATION

Ragland was all over the map during our Rock Hall talk. Here are some pointed excerpts. Imagine my surprise.

While people in Australia and Japan recognize the quality of Cleveland soul music, it's "virgin territory" in Cleveland, where radio continues to ignore it—same as it ever was.

"We could have been the next Motown here in this town, had we known that it was not the record business but the promotion, advertising and sales business," he said. "We could produce the product, but it was like having a light under a bush; nobody could see it. Plus we had to get past Berry Gordy, because in those days payola money was going around and they paid people more money not to play your record than it was for you to pay to get your record played.

"You couldn't get the product," he claimed. "If you had a hit record break out of Cleveland and tried to get it pressed somewhere, United Press would say, We can't get you in. Same in Detroit and Nashville." Boddie Recording would step into the breach but

only partially. WABQ wouldn't touch his music; it was too local. Only Ken Hawkins at WJMO championed Ragland's music.

"We don't have a Cleveland Sound. In Philadelphia, you got the Sound of Philadelphia. You got the Motown Sound. It's marketing—and style."

I didn't grasp the power of Lou Ragland until I met him at the Rock and Roll Hall of Fame in 2013. He was a solidly built man with a grizzled corona of hair, a warm voice and an undeniable presence.

I thought Lou would be guarded and defensive. On the contrary. Our talk at the Rock Hall, and our subsequent telephone conversations, were more than cordial. As our relationship developed, we began to discuss writing his biography. His death by cancer killed that. He lives on on Bandcamp and YouTube.

WATCH

In a nearly 90 minute interview on the stage of the Rock & Roll Hall of Fame auditorium, Carlo and Lou explored many previously unheard Invisible Soul stories.

12

Smooth, Smart & STYLISH

John S. Wilson's Sly, Slick & Wicked perseveres in the face of label turnover, unfortunate timing, and a group of nearly the same name stealing its thunder. Wilson's is a cautionary, inspiring tale.

WILLIAM WHITE AND WILLIAM HAIRSTON, owners of King's Men's Shop in Cleveland's Lee Road-Harvard Avenue area, struggled to keep the members of the vocal group the Tam-A-Las in stylish, affordable and well-tailored outfits. It was the early 1960s, and the performers weren't even in their teens when their first stage costumes were fitted.

Tam-A-Las founder John Wilson and confederates James Sizemore, Michael Johnstone, Irvin Holmes and Paul Woodhall, Wilson's buddies from Charles W. Eliot Junior High School, were only 12 when they formed their doo-wop group. To the men who discovered and advised them, it was clear that these talented kids needed clothes that fit as smoothly as their harmonies.

Named after the Motown label Tamla, the group progressed through several iterations during the 1960s, ultimately reducing to La Cockdors featuring Wilson and Harold Beverly on vocals, backed by child prodigy Clarence Gillespie of Little G and the Vibrators on drums, Joe Pearson on bass and George Jones on guitar. La Cockdors lasted three months in 1969 before Wilson, along with Charles Still and Madison "Marc" Saxton, formed The Mod Squad, a vocal trio backed by the La Cockdors rhythm section. As 1969 turned into 1970, the group solidified its format—and became Sly (Wilson), Slick (Still, still Slick after all these years) & Wicked (Saxton was the first of seven).

THE ROOTS

BILL MCCULLUM, A PROMOTER from Cincinnati who owned a barber shop on Lee at Eldamere Avenue next to King's Men's Clothing, was the right man at the right time. In the Tam-A-Las, McCullum recognized quality—or, rather, heard it— as Wilson's earliest group sang a cappella at the opening of another clothing store, at Lee and Seville roads. McCullum was a booking agent who hung around Harrell's Barber Shop, where Wilson and his friends got their hair cut. He regaled the boys with tales of the road including work with Frankie Lymon, the short-lived singer of "Why Do Fools Fall in Love" and a prototype for Michael Jackson. (Unlike Jackson, Lymon was essentially a one-hit wonder, dying of a heroin overdose when he was only 25.)

Harrell's was the go-to barber shop "and all of us used to gather there," recalls Wilson. Promoter McCullum's stories captivated the boys, and the shop had a yarnspinner bonus: One of the barbers was a former member of the Jarmels, a Richmond, Virginia group that hit in 1962 with "A Little Bit of Soap." (That novelty song was written by Bert Berns, who became famous for producing "Brown Eyed Girl," Van Morrison's 1967 smash.)

Encouraged by a teacher who allowed them to sing after class, coaxed by McCullum, and outfitted by the men of King's, the Tam-A-Las were ready to provide entertainment for the cabaret scene even though they were under age. The presence of alcohol at these cabaret parties was, let's say, unofficial.

"The Black community—this has been going on for many years—is where the phrase 'BYOB,' or bring your own bottle, came from," says Wilson. "You would have entertainment and pay $2 for a set-up, a bucket of ice and four cans of Coke, and you'd bring your bottle out." Since the 1920s, many such places without liquor licenses thrived in Cleveland's Black community, including in the Lee-Miles area where Wilson spent his adolescence. McCullum told the Tam-A-Las he wanted to hire them as entertainment for a cabaret party at what used to be known as Shaker Lee Hall on Lee Road near Euclid Avenue.

"We were fascinated," Wilson says. They sang doo-wop, "under the street lamp-style." The men of King's Men's Shop—co-owner Hairston was fatally shot in the store "in front of everyone," Wilson recalls—"put the clothes on us. They dressed us from 1962 to 1968."

"We got $5 apiece for the cabaret."

Tony Robinson, who worked at King's Men's Clothing, managed the Tam-A-Las and choreographed them. Robinson would later manage the Ponderosa Twins + One, a kiddie group with two sets of twins, designed to compete with the Jackson Five.

The Tam-A-Las broke up in 1968. Wages improved. Group names changed.

THE BLACK MUSIC NETWORK

THAT CABARET PARTY AT Shaker-Lee Hall where the Tam-A-Las performed took place two years before the first British Invasion. Motown was a young company, doo-wop hadn't yet grown into rhythm and blues, records were still made of shellac, and radio was AM only—and more segregated than today. At the same time, radio was wide open, not yet calcified into formula. And all kinds of independent record labels were spreading a diverse musical vernacular spanning country, blues, and the seeds of soul.

For Wilson, who grew up in a musical family, music was always around, and not just thanks to Cleveland's Black radio stations. Radio was actually in the air, or so it seemed to young Wilson.

"Ever hear about Randy?" he asks, plucking a name out of the ether. "As soon as WABQ would go off the air—it was 1540—you would turn the dial all the way down and Randy would come in through the atmosphere. You had Randy's Grab Bag and you could hear all the greatest r&b hits and get a whole bag of records and it would cost a dollar." Wilson sent Randy quite a few dollars.

WABQ was the key daytime Black station in Cleveland. WJMO its nighttime counterpart. WLAC, an influential Nashville station with a powerful signal, was at a whole other level. One of its DJs was Randy Wood, owner of Randy's Record Shop in nearby Gallatin, Tennessee. Wood was a mail-order pioneer and a warrior for Black music. Or at least a canny businessman who saw the growing Black listening audience as a commercial opportunity.

"If the atmosphere was right, you could get his show all the way up to New York," Wilson says. "It was just called Randy, and he was, like, the Alan Freed of this station. He would say, Send me your address and send me a dollar and I'll send you a whole bag of records. You didn't know what you were getting, but they were records. Remember, in the '50s there was no r&b, no country, no kind of chart like that. You'd have Little Richard there with Elvis and Elvis there with Frank Sinatra."

Chart stratification took a giant step in 1949 when Jerry Wexler, then a writer for the music-industry trade magazine *Billboard*, coined the term "rhythm and blues," changing the name of the magazine's "race records" chart. Wexler became a major musical and cultural influence as a producer for Atlantic Records, the pioneering r&b label.

"In the '60s, when they developed this, they were only dealing with what they called standard pop," Wilson says of the record charts. "The r&b circuit had been circulating for years. For example, all the Black stations all across the United States had their own network. That's how we worked, OK? All the Black stations were independent."

As were many recording operations. Wilson cites Boddie Recording Company, where everything Tom and Louise Boddie "built was actually stuck together with bubble gum. That's the way these radio stations were." The situation could be scary. "There was one interview we did down in Alabama," Wilson recalls. "When we got out of the car, the guy told us there was water, and if you didn't watch your step an alligator would come up and bite you."

A group's musical status didn't matter when it came to Black acts—including major ones like B.B. King and the Temptations—working "the chitlin' clubs and doing the chitlin' radio interviews."

Black radio stations effectively constituted their own network, Wilson says. WABQ was dawn to dusk, WJMO was on all night, and the stations would "talk" to each other. "Then they would also 'talk' to the record stores, and they would find out what was going on." Stations would contact record stores area by area to gauge activity, sharing the information beyond the Cleveland region. "And they would call WBLS in Chicago: We're playing Sly, Slick & Wicked. So the promoters would know how to book you and how to move you. Take a *Billboard* magazine from 1970 and you won't see that many Black acts on there. That's why."

Black acts laid the foundation, Wilson suggests. White acts got the glory.

He cites two vintage white acts as proof of that assertion: "Who was really accepted and who says to this day that if it

WHEN WE GOT OUT OF THE CAR, THE GUY TOLD US TO WATCH YOUR STEP—AN ALLIGATOR COULD COME UP AND BITE YOU.

wasn't for the Black Chitlin' Circuit radio they wouldn't have had a career was the Righteous Brothers," he says. "The Four Seasons, when they first came out, people thought they were Black."

EVOLUTION TRIO-STYLE

BETWEEN 1962 AND 1968, the Tam-A-Las played cabarets and talent shows in Cleveland, adhering to the three-vocalist/backup band format. In high school, Wilson says, the Tam-A-Las's backup was the original members of Bell Telefunk (or Bell Telephunk), the nucleus of what would come to be the Dazz Band, one of the few Cleveland-area acts to become nationally successful.

The Dazz Band warrants a book of its own. Its history is murky and controversial, with several people claiming to have founded it, battles over trademarking the brand, and different versions of its history and development. This is Wilson's take on its embryonic days.

Wilson attended then-brand-new John F. Kennedy High School on Harvard Avenue with Bell Telefunkers Kenny Brown, a founding member, on bass; Ed Brown, guitar; Johnny Poindexter, keyboards; Joel Jackson, guitar; and Sim "Doby" London, another founding member, on drums. Congas player Carlos Martinez, who Wilson says went on to work with Average White Band and the Temptations, was the only original Telefunker not from Cleveland. (London's parents, Sim and Blanch, were known as "Mr. and Mrs. 88 Keys," trading pianistics and vocals at the Mardi Gras and the Encore Room, Chagrin Boulevard clubs the couple owned. Sim Junior also contributed.)

Kenny and Ed Brown, Johnny Poindexter, Joel Jackson and Sim London are backup on "Stay My Love/Surely, Is You Is Or Is You Ain't My Baby," the first Sly, Slick & Wicked recording, a 45 RPM single Paramount Records released in

1972. The road to that release was long and winding.

After Wilson graduated from JFK in 1968, Tam-A-Las Michael Johnstone and Paul Woodhall quit (Woodhall joined the Out-Of-Sights, a group that recorded for local label Saru); Wilson then formed La Cockdors, doing his best Dave Prater vocals to former Tam-A-La Harold Beverly's best Sam Moore's. In 1969, after Beverly left to work with Ali "Ollie" Woodson (a future Temptation), Wilson formed the Mod Squad, naming the three-singer group after what was then the hippest show on television. That group recorded a live date at Boddie.

That Boddie date, which archival label Numero Group released decades later, signaled an end to Wilson's five-singer format. Credit Smoke, Heat & Fire for convincing him three singers was the way to go.

Smoke, Heat & Fire was a Detroit group originally known as the Fabulous Peps. "Somehow they drifted down to Cleveland and Jules Berger and Leo Frank at Leo's Casino picked them up and managed them, and changed their name from the Peps to Smoke, Heat & Fire," Wilson says. The O'Jays, the Temptations—and Wilson himself—all consider SH&F one of the best groups they've ever seen, Wilson says. A September 20, 1969 article in the *Call & Post* says Smoke, Heat & Fire was a show-stopper indeed and breathtakingly touted a three-week Leo's engagement for the trio.

Smoke, Heat & Fire often was compared to the Impressions and built a reputation for inventive and athletic dancing. Joe "Pep" Harris eventually left the group to join the Undisputed Truth, a Motown Records "psychedelic soul" band that lasted into the 1980s. Among that group's early-70s hits: "Smiling Faces Sometimes" and "What It Is."

The moves, the repartee, the singing made Smoke, Heat & Fire total entertainers. "When I went to see them, it completely changed my thinking," Wilson says.

SLY, SLICK & WICKED FIRMS UP

IN 1969 AND 1970, Wilson's groups—first the Mod Squad, then Sly, Slick & Wicked—performed all over the Chitlin' Circuit, mainly in the South. Toward the end of 1969, they toured as The Mod Squad, taking their cues from the more experienced Pearson. They hit clubs in Columbus and Youngstown, Ohio; Kentucky; Erie, Pennsylvania, and Buffalo, New York. In 1970, they were an opening act for soul singer Frank Cooper, and they traveled in style: Cooper, who played clubs in Cleveland in the mid-60s, including an English Grille bill with the multitalented Lou Ragland, drove a gray 1961 Cadillac limousine. Alabama also figured large in their itinerary, with dates in Huntsville, Mobile, and Bessemer.

In 1970, Kenny Brown, the Bell Telefunk bassist, hooked them up with Eddie Perrell, a soul singer who had a seven-inch 45 called "The Spoiler" out on Volt, an affiliate of the fabled Memphis label Stax. Perrell, who sounds like a smoother Otis Redding, changed the name of Wilson's group to Sly, Slick & Wicked and flew from New York to Cleveland to produce the first SS&W single, "Stay My Love/Shirley," at Motion Picture Sound, a studio on Payne Avenue. Tapes of the two sides (records then had A and B sides) in hand, Perrell contacted Dean Courtney, who worked in production for Black artists at Paramount Records. Courtney signed them to a deal, the single came out in 1972, and Sly, Slick & Wicked finally entered the mainstream.

The group recorded another single for Paramount, "It's not Easy/Your Love Was Meant for Me," but by that time,

the original Wicked had left; filling the Wicked slot has been an issue from the beginning. (The Wicked on "It's Not Easy" is Terrance Stubbs, the cousin of Levi Stubbs of the Four Tops.)

Recorded at Media Recording in New York, where Kool and the Gang was recording at the time, "It's Not Easy" did pretty well—at least at first. Unfortunately, Paramount was getting out of the record business. Besides, Paramount had only two soul acts: Sly, Slick & Wicked, and the Pointer Sisters, on the Paramount-distributed Blue Thumb label.

ENTER THE GODFATHER

EVEN AS PARAMOUNT WAS phasing out its record label, James Brown was looking into Sly, Slick & Wicked. "Unbeknownst to us, James Brown had his eye on us," Wilson says. "We didn't know at the time that he really liked us. As soon as our contract ran out with Paramount, we were immediately picked up by his personal label, People." People was Brown's custom label, distributed by the giant company Polydor.

The group—Wilson, Still and Stubbs—recorded their own tune "Sho' Nuff," backed by "Ready for You," by Alvin Taylor and Jimmy Norman. Produced by Perrell and the Godfather of Soul himself, the dreamy, creamy "Sho' Nuff" was arranged by Bert DeCoteaux, a famous producer who worked with everybody from Sister Sledge to the Main Ingredient to Albert King to B.B. King to jazz trumpeter Freddie Hubbard. It's a great track; even the spoken interlude feels organic. Part of the reason it locks in so tight is that the band was Brown's backup band Fred Wesley and the JBs—and Brown himself plays organ and

> **ON THAT BILL, I WALKED IN, AND THERE'S COUNT BASIE, B.B. KING, BOBBI HUMPHREY, CANNONBALL ADDERLEY, THE OHIO PLAYERS, NEW BIRTH, HAROLD MELVIN AND THE BLUE NOTES.**
>
> **FIRST TIME I EVER PLAYED IN FRONT OF 80,000 PEOPLE**

bells. In inviting SS&W to his label, Brown inducted them into what Brown called the "First Family of Soul." Other members of that select kinfolk included Wesley and the JBs, the commanding saxophonist Maceo Parker, and singer Lyn Collins.

Recorded at Advantage Studios in New York City, the song "ended up in the Top 10 on the Black radio charts and we ended up doing *Soul Train*," Wilson says. Produced by Perrell and Brown, the B side was "I'm Ready for You," a song Wilson didn't like but his mates did. "Ready" has become a favorite of fans of Northern Soul.

THE SEVENTIES A MIXED BAG FOR SS&W

DURING THIS DECADE, SLY, Slick & Wicked became ever more popular. At the same time, they were never secure on the label front.

They began the decade on Paramount, had a tantalizing and rewarding experience on James Brown's People imprint, got a big push from the O'Jays, were distributed by Motown for a year, and wound up briefly on Sweet City, the Cleveland-based label that also was home to the seriously popular white funk group Wild Cherry and to Samona Cooke, daughter of the iconic, tragic singer Sam Cooke. Distributed by Epic Records, Sweet City was part of the powerful, Cleveland-based Belkin-Maduri organization.

Two dates stand out for Wilson as high points: a *Soul Train* appearance and a giant concert at Kauffman Stadium in Kansas City, Missouri. "Soul Train" was a highly popular, syndicated TV show that ran from 1971 to 2006. Producer Don Cornelius called People/Polydor and "requested us to be on his show," Wilson says. "*Soul Train* only booked the top acts for the show."

That *Soul Train* date of Sept. 15, 1973 ranks—nearly—with a date that same year when Sly, Slick & Wicked performed at the KOOL Jazz Festival in Kansas City. (George Wein's KOOL Jazz Festivals, descendants of the Newport Jazz Festival Wein debuted in 1954, came to present a blend of jazz, funk and soul in multi-day events. They ran until 2007.)

"The one that will always stick out in my mind is when we played Kansas City," Wilson says. "On that bill, I walked in, and there's Count Basie, B.B. King, Bobbi Humphrey, Cannonball Adderley, the Ohio Players, New Birth, Harold Melvin and the Blue Notes. First time I ever played in front of 80,000 people.

"These are the people my parents talked about and here I am on a show with them," Wilson says, still marveling. "New Birth, the Ohio Players, Isley Brothers, they were on the show, too, and that's fine, because I was working with them every day. But my point is, when I'm sitting there with Count Basie and with Cannonball Adderley and Freddie Hubbard and B.B. King—that's a whole different ball game. I was in awe. I was feeling like, I'm here, but can I really believe it? I'm being accepted in this crowd—these great men, you know?

"The Kansas City Royals Stadium was packed," he says. "In the *Saxman* movie (a 2014 documentary about SS&W backup saxophone player and Cleveland figure Maurice Reedus), you see Maurice waving to me as we were walking in, and we got a standing ovation when we walked off the stage. That's probably the high point. That and doing *Soul Train*. *Soul Train*, when we did it, was the No. 1 TV show in the world. I had a wonderful time."

"Sho' Nuff" has had quite an afterlife. Not only did its success vault the group onto *Soul Train*, the white soul singer Justin Timberlake sampled it for his 2013 hit "Suit & Tie," and Anheuser Busch sampled it for a beer commercial. Sly, Slick & Wicked sued Timberlake, claiming Timberlake's record company had paid Universal Music Group, which absorbed James Brown's People label, to use the music from "Sho' Nuff," but not the vocals. The Timberlake case is ongoing; the Anheuser Busch case was settled out of court.

The sampling disputes aren't Wilson's only headache. He's also dealing with people trading on and profiting from his band's name without having any relationship to the real thing.

Google Sly, Slick & Wicked and you'll likely land on allmusic.com, a virtual encyclopedia of musician biographies, song lists and samples. The site offers two Sly, Slick & Wicked biographies, one of the original and one of a Los Angeles-based group that trademarked the name as Sly, Slick and Wicked—spelling out the ampersand. The original group got its trademark back about three years ago, Wilson says, but the fake iteration continues to tour—as does the real thing.

There are fake Blue Magics, Wilson says. There are fake O'Jays. No doubt there will be more counterfeit groups as the originals age out, because names have power, names draw. The issues such rogue competition raises strike at the heart of legitimate commerce and identity.

What will happen when all the original members of a group have died, leaving behind only the name? What makes such rootless bands anything other than cover or tribute bands?

To prevent such fakery, Wilson allied with Jon "Bowzer" Bauman of the group Sha Na Na and the late Mary Wilson of the Supremes to push the Truth in Music Advertising act, a bill adopted by most states. The legislation, which Wilson wants federalized, says there must be at least one original member of a group active for the group to use its original name. The aim is to protect the livelihood of members of original groups like Sly, Slick & Wicked, Sha Na Na, the Drifters and Fleetwood Mac.

LABEL TROUBLE

"SHO' NUFF" TURNED OUT to be Sly, Slick & Wicked's only People release, and the group began to look for another label. The People label ceased operation in 1976.

In 1974, wondering where they would land, they learned that the O'Jays were starting a record label—in Cleveland. The two groups go way back.

"The O'Jays will always be in my heart as some of our greatest friends … and one of the greatest groups," Wilson says, namechecking the original lineup of Walter Williams, Eddie Levert, William Powell, Bobby Massey and Will Isles. "They've always been there for us, to this day."

The O'Jays were especially busy that year, working with the Philadelphia International label, founding the O'Jays Production Company at a former doctors' office building around East 126th Street and Miles Avenue, and starting their own label, Shaker Records. That same year, they released 45s by Sly, Slick & Wicked and by keyboardist Bobby Dukes and vocalist Cynthia Woodard. After Woodard made that record with Dukes, a regular O'Jays sideman, she left town to join the Blossoms, backup singers for Welsh soulman Tom Jones.

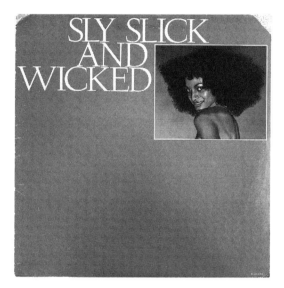

The group's self-titled album, published by Detroit's Ju-Par Records in 1977

These are the only Shaker Records singles. The label lasted only a year, forcing Sly, Slick & Wicked to seek out yet another record industry home.

The O'Jays promoted Sly, Slick & Wicked's 45, "We Don't Have To Be Lovers /Turn on Your Lovelight," heavily, but airplay was confined to Black stations. The group continued to perform, gracing the stages of Cleveland clubs such as the Habachi Lounge and Sir-Rah's House.

In 1975, Sly, Slick & Wicked found themselves without a label again. Enter Motown.

THE BIG TIME

THAT YEAR, A NEW York-based producer named Roy Norman called Wilson to see whether Sly, Slick & Wicked wanted to record for Ju-Par Records, a new Motown affiliate label founded by Detroit businessmen John "Juney" Garrett and Richard Parker. In 1977, the only year it enjoyed Motown distribution, Ju-Par released albums by SS&W, the Ju-Par Universal Orchestra, and Flavor. It also released singles by that Orchestra and Flavor, but not Sly, Slick & Wicked.

In 1976, Norman flew to Cleveland and arranged a deal in which O'Jays Eddie Levert and Walter Williams would produce half the SS&W album, Norman the other half. Recording was split between Agency Recording in Cleveland (with famed engineer Arnie Rosenberg) and Newcastle, a studio on Long Island, New York, Wilson says. The album did well enough to put SS&W on tour with the O'Jays, the Dramatics, and New Birth. It did even more—until momentum stalled again.

"It was doing so well, Motown pulled us off the road and wanted us to start recording another album, so we moved to New York and this time Roy was doing the whole album," Wilson recalls. That LP remains unreleased; it was stopped dead in its tracks when label co-founder Garrett "got killed somewhere down in Florida," prompting Motown to pull the plug on Ju-Par.

Sly, Slick & Wicked wasn't out of gas, however. A casual encounter led to yet another record deal. In 1977, SS&W signed with Sweet City Records, a Cleveland label distributed by Epic Records. Formed by legendary Midwest music figures Mike Belkin and Carl Maduri, Sweet City was riding high behind Wild Cherry's smash, "Play That Funky Music."

Wilson told Maduri the group was still performing "but we're looking for another label. He said, Why don't you come to my label? We're having a lot of success with Wild Cherry. I said I'd be glad to. We ended up signing with Carl."

Produced and arranged by Dunn Pearson Jr., who also worked with the O'Jays (and is Wilson's cousin), SS&W recorded Pearson's "All I Want Is You/The Prophet." The A side—driving and layered and pretty, largely because of Wilson's lead vocal—got mostly pop airplay and "still did very well for us," Wilson says. But its 1979 release did not lead to an album.

It led to something else.

"Carl said, Hey, man, I would really like to cut something on you, and I said, Really? Me? Yeah, let me try something on you. You got anything?"

Wilson came up with "Ain't Enough Lovin'," written with Sharon Pate of Silk, Satin & Lace. Wilson flew out to Los Angeles,

2023 promo shot of John "Sly" Wilson, Charles "Slick" Still and Masta "Wicked" Edwards

recorded the tune in Pate's boyfriend's studio, and flew it back to Cleveland so Maduri could hear it. He loved it and, backed by the instrumental, "Moody Feeling," released it on Sweet City in 1980. "The only time I ever went single," Wilson says.

He should have gone single more often. "Ain't Enough Lovin'" is supple, inviting and, thanks to a taut bass line and Wilson's easy vocal, very danceable. By that time, Wilson had left his hometown for the Los Angeles area; the blizzard of 1978, marked by freezing rain and stratospheric winds, was the last Cleveland straw.

SPREADING HIS WINGS

OVER THE YEARS, WILSON has produced some notable Black artists, including the latter-day Impressions and LaToya Jackson. His production work had an auspicious start.

When J.J. Johnson, a DJ friend, brought Wilson to a party in the Sherman Oaks neighborhood of Los Angeles, Wilson could tell he was getting into something good, or at least something ritzy. The Rolls Royce in the driveway was a sign.

Turns out the house belonged to Barry White, the boudoir baritone who sashayed his way through such hits as "Never Never Gonna Give Ya Up" and "You're The First, The Last, My Everything."

"You ever thought about becoming a producer?" White, who was hip to Sly, Slick & Wicked, asked Wilson. "I would love to become a producer," Wilson said, whereupon White said, "I want you up to my house every day."

Wilson ended up working on two Barry White albums, *Beware!* and *Barry & Glodean*. He is not credited as a producer but is named in the "special thanks," as Wilson was just getting "my feet wet."

HONORS AND AUTHENTICITY

WILSON HAS BEEN HONORED. He's been inducted into the National Rhythm & Blues Hall of Fame, an organization established in 2013 that stages induction ceremonies in various places, mostly Detroit. Sly, Slick & Wicked were inducted into the Motown Alumni Association Hall of Fame in 2003. A Sly, Slick & Wicked display became part of a permanent Ohio musical talent exhibit at the Rock and Roll Hall of Fame in Cleveland in 2004. The California city of San Bernardino awarded Wilson a certificate of merit in 2020. People have been clamoring for reissues of the Ju-Par album and the various singles. They also request the issuance of unreleased songs Wilson developed with the O'Jay Walter Williams.

Is he a success? "I feel like I've done some things, but it ain't over yet," Wilson says. "There's still more I'd like to do. I consider myself blessed."

Deep down, he's still the talented, little kid who delighted his family with his trumpet prowess. "I want people to know that I tried to do the best I could to make people happy," Wilson says.

"I never made a song I couldn't play for my mother."

Epilogue | FREE MY SOUL

AT THE SAME TIME *INVISIBLE SOUL* WAS bubbling under, my wife and I began talking about leaving the suburbs. That conversation quickened when the pandemic hit, and in April 2121, with COVID-19 at its peak, we made the move—to Cleveland. It was a difficult and very conscious decision, and I'm glad we made it. *Invisible Soul* affirms my commitment to, and belief in, a city I've come to love.

Not that I disliked South Euclid, an inner-ring suburb east of Cleveland where we raised two girls who are now adults. I still like it, and I miss the convenience and abundance of the East Side suburbs. It pisses me off that my local supermarket doesn't carry sushi, a suburban commonplace. Such a First World problem.

Living in this city of character, personality and history comes with its own joys: Engaging with the family next door, familiarizing yourself with distinctive neighborhoods, learning your way around, stumbling on secrets like a terrific, inner-city meat market.

One of the most engaging things about Cleveland is that its history is visible, the old buildings and vacant lots almost eager to tell stories. Where we live is close to wherever we want to go, and the streets, built when Cleveland had a lot more people and traffic, hasten and facilitate the journey. Another pleasure for me is getting involved politically in a city that badly needs such connections. (It helps that our move overlapped a Cleveland regime change, as the progressive Justin Bibb succeeded perpetual incumbent Mayor Frank Jackson).

While the city's population continues to drop—3,782 fewer people were living in Cleveland in July 2022, a 1-percent drop to a total of 368,000—the rate of loss seems to be slowing, according to data from the Census Bureau. The previous year, the loss was 6,428, likely a reflection of the first year of the pandemic.

There is so much to do right in—and by—Cleveland. Lifting it out of poverty is key. So is civic engagement that drives voter turnout, which requires a better-educated population. Gun violence keeps the city on edge, chronic racial and geographic divides need bridging, and political will must be first nurtured and then mobilized to expand on the promise I feel living in a development that's integrated, gender-neutral—and tolerant, without preachiness or sanctimoniousness. This timeless 1968 lyric from Sly and the Family Stone's "Everyday People" encapsulates what I've done with Invisible Soul.

> *There is a blue one who can't accept*
> *The green one for living with*
> *A fat one tryin' to be a skinny one*
> *Different strokes for different folks*
> *And so on and so on and scooby-dooby-dooby*
> *We got to live together*

Invisible Soul is a valentine to an era I lived through—elsewhere—without knowing its significance. Life goes on as history accumulates, history takes a long time, and meaning arrives even later.

Writing about a bygone Cleveland opened a weirdly familiar world to me. It also presented challenges in research and organization. As I marshaled my resources and mined sources to put this together, my writing adapted and expanded to reach that goal. I began to see this project in a more imaginative, less journalistic light.

I'm not "objective" here, as journalism dictates. But I'm true to my subjects, be they key musicians from that era or the changing fortunes of the city of Cleveland itself. Truth, backed by facts, has been my goal here.

I chose to end this book with another Sly: John "Sly" Wilson, the head of a group he founded more than 50 years ago. Sly, Slick & Wicked keeps performing, battling an impostor band of a very similar name and raising several questions: What happens when all the original band members

My interview with Abdul Ghani was one of my most dynamic. Interactive and enjoyable, too.

have died? Who owns the name of the band? Is a band with no original members anything but a cover band?

In November 2022, Alphonso Boyd, a founder of Cleveland's Imperial Wonders, went on tour in Thailand as a member of the multiply incarnated Platters. The tour was to resume in September 2023 for 15 dates in South America. Boyd also leads the tribute band "Al Boyd's Men of Motown" and "Al Boyd's Tribute To The Delfonics." God love him for perpetuating voices of Invisible Soul.

Stories of electric times and electrifying places make me wish I'd been there, and I'm eager to present glimpses of a period when fissures that continue to deepen began to crack segregation. That complex story will never be complete.

CARLO WOLFF

B-SIDES

The byproduct of my work is often haunting. That's especially true of Invisible Soul. A few years thinking and more than a dozen years interviewing, writing, and editing unearthed far more material than I could ever fit into this 9" x 9" volume. These stories, and the personalities behind them, have become friends.

What follows are a few favorites that I've been able to bring to life in a tighter, less formal way. Like the "B-sides" of 45-rpm records, they may not be the top 10 hits that the public swoons for and publishers crave. But they're special to me. Hope you like them.

And if you have a B-side story of your own that makes Cleveland's Invisible Soul special, send it to me for possible inclusion online or in a future print run. —CW

1 SMOKEY STABBING

The group was Smokey Robinson and the Miracles, and Carter Playground in Boston's South End was packed. It was summer 1968. The free show was part of Summerthing, an entertainment program created by Boston Mayor Kevin White that continued into the 1970s. Summerthing gave young people something to do during those long, hot summers, when riots rocked many American cities.

My girlfriend and I, part of the white minority at the event, grooved to these paragons of Motown royalty. Out of nowhere, a young Black guy, flanked by friends, pulled a knife and demanded my money. For a split second, I was defiant; that pissed him off.

In a blink, he stabbed me in the chest. I gave him my money. I was in shock. So was Susan. I couldn't drive, so Susan drove us to the emergency room at Peter Bent Brigham.

In that sweaty room, my attitude toward drugs crystallized: Stop fighting the drug wars. I think drugs of all kinds should be controlled and, on a case-by-case basis, accessible for both pleasure and medical reasons.

Back in that emergency room, I told them I was in pain, as if my bleeding wasn't sufficient evidence. I requested pain killers, which they didn't give me because I told them I was on methadone, a synthetic opiate prescribed to me through a program at Boston State Hospital in Mattapan. What struck me about that situation was they were more willing to keep me in pain than relieve it. I still resent that.

At least they treated my wound, bound me up and sent me home.

2 THERE GOES THE NEIGHBORHOOD

"At one time, Black folks didn't have a lot of people to look up to," says Abdul Sunni Ghani, born Edward Lee Williams Jr. in Atlanta. "You had your Joe Louises and Sugar Ray Robinsons, you know what I mean?" he says, recalling the late '50s and early '60s, when this talented adolescent sang in doo-wop groups including the El Deons and the Sensations.

"In the neighborhood, when you came in looking at

people who might be successful, most of them were hustlers and pimps, running around in their fancy cars; their shoes were clean. They had some Black entrepreneurs back then—Art's Seafood and a couple of other spots, like Dearing's Restaurant."

But starting in the 1950s, whole neighborhoods were relocated, pawns on massive urban renewal chess boards.

"When I moved into East Cleveland in 1966—these are my feelings—East Cleveland was one of the so-called suburbs to open up to let Blacks move in; it was mostly white, but it had a sprinkle of Blacks. People tried to relocate to get away from certain things. East Cleveland eventually became the new ghetto, and it looks like a war zone," he says.

3 NEIGHBORHOOD SCHOOLING

Every Friday and Saturday night, Tom King and the Starfires played the Dove Lounge on East 116th Street and Dove Avenue. Jimmy Fox was the Starfires's drummer; the Dove Lounge clientele was largely white. Just up 116th was the Pin Wheel Lounge, with Black clientele. "The house band at the Pin Wheel at that time was Don Gregory and the Montclairs," recalls Fox. "They were a terrific group with excellent players at every instrument. They played a bit later than we did, so every night for months, we would leave the stage at the Dove at 2:30 in the morning and run the 50 yards or so over to the Pin Wheel to catch as much of the last set from the Montclairs as we could. The drummer was a man named Jack Cooper and I was totally in awe of him. He played with such style and funk that I could hardly stand it and I seldom took my eyes off of him while they were playing. I recall his playing style very well, even close to 60 years later, and at the time, I wanted to play like he did. I think that every member of our band felt there was a lot to be learned from every member of their band, and besides, listening to them was just so much fun. Those formative years were great!"

Jimmy Fox would soon join the Outsiders of "Time Won't Let Me" fame. In 1966, Fox founded the James Gang, a hard-rock trio that won international acclaim. Jackie Cooper became the drummer for the O'Jays.

4 THE FACE OF ENTERTAINMENT

Freddie Arrington made quite a mark on Cleveland's Black entertainment scene as the face of Leo's Casino, the city's premier Black-and-tan nightclub. He made comedian Flip Wilson, jazz organist Jimmy Smith and many other stars comfortable at Leo's and the other clubs that gave the area known as 105 its too-fleeting cachet.

"Entertainers gave me a job because I didn't upstage them," Arrington told me in April 2011. "I build them up so they are somebody. They're the star, the big wheel."

Arrington's family moved to Cleveland from New York City when Freddie—one of 10 children— was 8. The family first lived on 97th Street off Cedar Road, moving to 83rd Street and Central Avenue, and finally to 128th and Kinsman Road.

"We lived by the railroad tracks, train come by, wake my father up, couldn't get back to sleep," he recalled. "My mother and father were two fantastic people. He didn't do no wrong and couldn't stand anybody else to do no wrong."

Arrington first deployed his sociability talent at Outhwaite Homes at East 43rd and Quincy Avenue, where brothers Louis and Carl Stokes also lived (Louis became a 15-term congressman; Carl was the first Black mayor of a major US city, Cleveland). When Arrington was a kid, he and a buddy formed a comedy duo to amuse folks at the public housing project's community center, extending their reach to different halls around town.

"People would have different parties at Outhwaite Homes," Arrington recalled. "We'd do an adult show and just a comedy act. We didn't get nasty or dirty, but the jokes could go either way."

Arrington attended Quincy Elementary School, Rawlings Junior High School and Central Senior High, but didn't graduate. Instead, he went into the service in 1951. He served in Korea and mustered out in 1956. He spent the next 20 years in Cleveland entertainment, counting Leo's owners Leo Frank and Jules Berger among his friends. They weren't his first entertainment connections.

Arrington became friends with the unique jazz balladeer "Little" Jimmy Scott when both were teens. Scott, who died in 2014, was five years older than Arrington.

Chickens brought them together. Arrington met Scott when "Little" Jimmy delivered chickens to a grocery store at 83rd and Central where Arrington worked.

It was a different world. Arrington's family raised chickens in its backyard, too, and one could buy baby chicks at places like Sears, Roebuck and Woolworth's. "That's a thousand years from what we're doing now," said Arrington, who remembers when refrigerators were ice boxes and people collected their milk from window boxes. "In those days, your telephone was a party line."

In 1977, well after Leo's closed, he moved to Los Angeles, prompted by his late wife Johnnie. He worked at the Post Office, retiring in 1993. No matter where he lived, however, Arrington maintained his ties to entertainment.

In Los Angeles, Arrington mounted some stage shows with Reynaldo Rey, a light-skinned, freckled man with reddish hair and a former Cleveland teacher who for a time worked at Karamu House. Rey also toured with the O'Jays. He wound up as a character actor. Arrington also worked with Sherman Helmsley, famous as George Jefferson in Norman Lear's popular 1970s sitcom, The Jeffersons.

In his pre-entertainment days, Arrington recalled, Jimmy Scott delivered chickens to a grocery at 83rd and Central where Arrington worked. He conjured a vanished, feathered and bloody world, one more palpable and dangerous but far less sanitary than today's. Scott abandoned those squawking fowl to become a unique jazz vocalist. Arrington, meanwhile, burrowed deep into entertainment.

In that old day, the Central Market around Ontario Street and Carnegie Avenue (the area now known as Gateway) was still thriving.

"In every neighborhood there was a chicken market," Arrington said. "You could go in and pick out the chicken you wanted. Live."

In the mid-50s, people were closer to the land than they are today, and there simply was more land, even in cities. Frozen food became popular, standardizing that kind of meal and giving consumers more options, and between 1950 and 1970, the number of people on farms declined from 20 million to 10 million.

Who knew that two kids from Cleveland's inner city would make such marks on the entertainment world? Birds of a feather in the geographical sense, friends starting when they were young, Freddie Arrington and Jimmy Scott refused to stay stuck in the coop.

5 A VOICE LIKE A WOUND

Jimmy Scott was a unique talent whose recordings go in and out of fashion.

Known for his oddly feminine, contralto voice—the consequence of Kallmann's syndrome, a hormonal deficiency that effectively trapped him in puberty—Scott specialized in the ballad. He sang behind the beat, slowing the listener down into contemplation. His was the voice of hurt.

After touring the southern chitlin' circuit with shake dancer Estelle "Caledonia" Young from 1943 to 1945, Scott rose to fame in the 1950s as a featured vocalist with the Lionel Hampton Band.

He recorded for various labels, primarily Savoy; several

stiffed him or at least under-promoted him. In 1992, largely thanks to the legendary producer Tommy LiPuma, like Scott a Cleveland native, Scott recorded *All the Way*, his first major-label album in 20 years.

A contemporary of other Cleveland natives like the trumpeter Benny Bailey and the in-demand pianist and arranger Willie Smith, Scott found a second wind with *All the Way*, a lush album that succeeded both commercially and critically. He continued recording into the new century.

Hard to categorize, unmistakable and moving, Scott made soul visible. He died in 2014.

6 EDDIE BROWN

Eddie Brown, white-bearded and snazzily hatted, was one of my earliest interviews for this book. We talked on February 20, 2011 at Tucker's Casino, a long-standing East Cleveland nightclub.

Brown was a member of the Imperial Wonders, a popular, Temptations-styled group of the late 1960s and early '70s. He also was in the original Bell Telefunk Company, which backed a lot of headliners at Leo's Casino, most notably the O'Jays. The jazz-fusion group Bell Telefunk evolved into the Dazz Band.

Like many other Invisible Soul musicians, Brown moved from group to group. So did Augustus "Gus" Hawkins, the hard-charging saxophonist and flutist who first came to prominence in S.O.U.L. (Sounds of Unity and Love).

Brown said he also worked with jazz artists such as saxophonist Eddie Harris and vibraharpist Roy Ayers. Venues where he played spanned the Sir-Rah House on Lee Road, Dearing's on Superior Avenue, and Tucker's Casino and the Eastown Hotel, both on Euclid Avenue in East Cleveland.

Brown was born in Junction City, Arkansas on June 25, 1950. The Browns moved to Cleveland when Eddie was 4, occupying a home on Franklin Avenue on the city's West Side. Brown experienced his first symbiosis with a guitar at that house.

The family shortly relocated to Garden Valley, a public housing project built in the '50s in Kingsbury Run, a Cleveland gully that was the burial site for the 12 Torso Murders, a string of serial killings in the 1930s. Garden Valley was new then and Cleveland wasn't altogether urban yet.

"It was country—you could ride up Kinsman, see chickens and stuff," Brown said.

In the mid-50s, when civil rights were still confined to the military, Black preachers were short on churches and held services at their congregants' homes. Brown conjured just such a scene at his Franklin Avenue home. He was 4 or 5.

"This week, church would be at Mrs. Jones' house. Next week, church was at Mrs. Smith's house. One week, church came to Mrs. Brown's house," he recalled. "I was standing in front of this amplifier and there were three singers, with one guy playing guitar whom I knew. The light on the amplifier put me in a daze and I just stood there; the gaze from that Fender was a brilliant light, and I asked him, Jesse, can I play your guitar? He gave me an acoustic guitar that I could play overnight. It was so big and I was so small that when I strummed the guitar, a feeling went through my heart. It took me a lifetime to figure out why it saddened me."

Largely self-taught, Brown has a natural ear for music and realized early on that a guitar is tuned in fourths, the first intervals of a bugler's "Taps." After he learned some music theory, he connected the sorrow his guitar expressed to "Taps" because that eulogy music "related to death."

Maybe a year after Jesse loaned him a guitar, Brown was at the dentist's for a tooth extraction. He had a dream while he was under.

"I was floating in air. It was dark all around. I could see myself floating there, with a golden harp laying upon my body and a white horse upon the harp. I could feel the strings pressing me and it was too heavy for me to push off. It was like a sandwich. It wasn't hurting, but it was uncomfortable, and I tried to push it off but I couldn't. I think it meant I would reach high in my music."

The harp represented the music. The horse represented the power structure.

As an adult, Brown could look back at that oppressive dream harp and connect it to the way "the guitar saddened me when I strummed it. I knew I was going to make something of this music."

7 COLORBLIND CANADA

In the late 1950s, Cleveland doo-wop group the Five Quails needed to fly north to really take off. Much of their flight was navigated by Harvey Fuqua, a Motown power-to-be. Good years, good times, and good stories followed.

From 1955 to 1976, the group hustled, from private "dawn dances" to clubs like Gleason's Music Bar, the Bandbox, and the Blackstone Café. The Five Quails even landed in New York's fabled Apollo Theater. It was the era of "bird bands."

Groups like the Swallows, the Ravens, the Penguins, and other doo-woppers were in vogue. Five Quails second tenor Billy Strawbridge explained the approach. "If you did something up-tempo, it was just to offset all your slow stuff. The slow, meaningful kinds of music at that time told a story," he said.

Courtesy of the chitlin' circuit, Strawbridge met a Toronto-based agent who booked Black acts throughout Canada. Each club supplied a backup band, but those Canadians needed coaching. "We had to teach the drummer what a backbeat was," Strawbridge said.

Headliners needed rhythm lessons, too. In the late '50s, the Quails opened for then-teen idol Pat Boone. "He couldn't even snap his fingers," said Strawbridge. "He could sing, but he had no rhythm."

Off tour, the Five Quails found their own rhythm in the '60s. The orchestrator of much of their success was Fuqua.

Strawbridge first met him on a southern tour with Fuqua's Moonglows and

Clyde McPhatter. Fuqua became the Five Quails manager, with plans to cut a record on Fuqua's label. Before Fuqua committed them to wax, however, they traveled to Houston to record for Don Robey's Peacock Records, home to Bobby 'Blue' Bland and other blues legends.

Robey "wanted 100 percent of everything," Strawbridge said. So the Five Quails balked, and the recordings were never released. From Texas, the Quails headed to New York and brighter results. At the Apollo Theater's Amateur Night, the group became the first to win that talent show six weeks in a row. The Quails—the "five" was often dropped in billing—also opened there in 1957 for the unruly Jerry Lee Lewis. Chuck Willis, the "King of the Stroll," caught that show and offered a spot on tour with him. That same year, a Philadelphia disc jockey hooked the Quails up with Mercury Records.

"We did seven or eight songs; they released two 45s and both of them did fairly well," said Strawbridge. When lead singer Harold Sudberry returned from military service in 1958, the group began its Canadian tours and in 1959 signed with Fuqua's Tri-Phi label. The connection led to three singles on sister label Harvey. Their tunes got airplay, and the Quails did well financially. In Canada and Cleveland they were at the top of their game.

"We were smooth, we had a lot of routines," said Strawbridge. "During those years, you had to be able to sell yourself and the song, you had to be a topnotch doo-wop group, you had to have good harmony, good moves and a good novelty routine. We had all of that."

8 WOLF'S DEN

Maybe eight years ago, a friend invited me to join him at a Cedar Road nightclub that was one of those rare joints that still presented live music. When I got there, no friend—and I felt very white. But I'm curious. I recognized some of the names of members of the band playing there and learned that the drummer was the son of the band leader. That they had different last names puzzled me. I've always had a thing with names, as mine is often misspelled (Carl O'Wolf does not scan), so I began asking around. All of a sudden, a woman rushed up and started bitching me out. She was the drummer's wife, and she was defending her man loudly and intimidatingly. It was a nerve-wracking scene.

It seems that in a Black club, you don't inquire into someone's lineage, particularly if you're a total, white stranger. I never did get an explanation for the name discrepancy. I was strongly persuaded to leave, which I did.

I've never felt so tone-deaf.

9 HAWKINS & HOPKINS

I was in my late teens when I first encountered jazz and blues. I was a student at Brandeis University, a school in the Boston suburb of Waltham, where my father chaired the sociology department. I didn't want to go to Brandeis—my preference was the University of Chicago—but I didn't buck my parents. Brandeis was a fine school, but I was a terrible student, failing classes in sullen rebellion. I was moody and broody, avoiding homework by feeding the student union jukebox. Thanks to me, the Booker T. and the M.G.'s instrumental "Green Onions" played over and over. I bet I wore out that 45.

Still, two performances stand out. I experienced the great saxophonist Coleman Hawkins at the student union, and the legendary Texas bluesman Lightnin' Hopkins at Cholmondeley's, a cozy coffee house at Brandeis. The Hopkins date was particularly resonant, more for the venue than the music.

Cholmondeley's is located in the basement of Usen Castle, a structure as bizarre as it was sturdy. Sixty years ago, an early girlfriend of mine, a senior, lived in one of Usen's upper floors. We spent a lot of time at her place, but several months into our torrid affair, she cooled off. That gave me a bad case of the blues. Listening to Lightnin' Hopkins, performing in the building where she lived, helped dull my pain.

10 THE BISHOP

His lifelong gift of counseling and salvaging the souls of the needy and the lost earned the Rev. John Burris Hicks Sr. this moniker: the Bishop.

Hicks boasted a strong, musical voice and a versatile touch on keyboards. He was persuasive, too, particularly when speaking of the Lord. A jack of musical trades, he created several record labels, including the secular imprint Del-Nita (inspired by his daughters, Del Laura and Bernita) and the gospel imprint Celestial. He also wrote gospel songs, including "I Thank the Lord"; "I'm So Happy in Jesus"; "God Is the Answer"; and "I Shall Overcome."

The first shellac Hicks produced was a gospel 78 committed to tape at Schneider Recording Studio on Prospect Avenue. Del-Nita also published a small group of 45s, most recorded at the Bishop's Hicks Recording Company at 6501 Euclid Avenue. The building also housed the Hicks Music Company and Hicks Record Store .

Hicks bought records wholesale from Dean's House of Jazz on Hough Avenue near Wade Park. He sold all kinds of records and recorded all kinds of groups.

Among the rarest Del-Nitas: "We Got It/Erebian-Borialis," a 45 the Night People released in 1967. "We Got It" is aggressive rock in the vein of mid-60s hit-makers the Standells (remember "Dirty Water?") and the Shadows of Knight ("Gloria.")

Other Del-Nita 45s included a pair of tunes by Friendly Womack Jr. (older brother to Bobby Womack, who struck it rich when the Rolling Stones covered Bobby's "It's All Over Now"), and a distant Hicks relative, Gene Allison; cuts by ethereal doo-woppers the Elements and the Inner Circles; and tracks by the remarkable Dottye Ramm, a heart-rending vocalist whose "Where Did You Stay Last Night" sends blues chills down your spine. Playing piano behind Ramm: the tune's composer, Leodis Harris, a fan of jazz-pop pianist Ramsey Lewis, who served for decades as Cuyahoga County juvenile judge.

While Hicks was an ecumenical musical bishop, at his core he was a producer. Whether he recorded a track at his studio or elsewhere, like Boddie, Hicks engineered a way to get it done.

In his role as financial backstop, Hicks fronted funds for engineering and studio time. "Back then, it was roughly $50 an hour," he told me in 2012 . "But now when you get into multi-track, it can go up to $500 an hour."

Tom Boddie and Cleveland Recording Company co-owner Ken Hamann used to buy parts from Hicks at Pioneer Electronics at East 55th Street and Prospect Avenue. Hicks also bought gear for his own studio from Pioneer, and Tom Boddie did a lot of repairs for Hicks.

Hicks remained close to home while dreaming of a bigger stage. In 1967, he traveled to Detroit to see whether he could break into Motown. "I wanted to get on the inside and learn the tricks of the trade. I didn't even get to first base," he said. After that fruitless trek, he discovered he'd talked to an attorney for Berry Gordy's hermetic operation. Not the best gateway.

A Ravenna native, Hicks came from a time when soul and spirituality coexisted easily and Cleveland's Black middle class was coming into its own. The sharing of interests seemed natural. So did the merging of styles.

"She had that projection," Hicks said of the haunting singer Dottye Ramm. "I'm talking about that soul projection. And that soul projection comes through experience." And from having people like the versatile, open-minded Hicks to spread the word.

The Bishop died on December 20, 2020. He was 86.

11 NO ROOM FOR COOTIES

"We didn't have Motown. Maybe we didn't have the resources. We were all little pockets of cats, like the Hesitations, Imperial Wonders, S.O.U.L.—little pockets of cats that did their own thing; white cats, too, like Bocky and the Visions (a popular '60s group that bridged rock and doo-wop).

"It wasn't about competition, because there was enough room to do their own thing. Wasn't nobody getting in your way."

"There was a point in time where you could start at St. Clair at 105 on foot and damn near walk to Euclid and run into a club on every corner, and they were playing jazz trios, organ trios with either a guitar or a tenor, and a drummer.

"Here's what was cool about those days. White people would come to these clubs and never be bothered by the thugs. There's always an element of criminal, but for some reason, the music was like an umbrella, like a ticket of admission, because there's an unwritten law among the thugs and the cooties: Don't mess with the patrons. It's true. So you'd see a white lady get out with a fur outside a Black club, the cat's all sharp with his hat—a white guy—and the cooties be out there, they part like the Red Sea. Cooties are thugs, stickup men, b&e guys. There was always a lot of them hanging out on the corner."

Trumpeter extraordinaire Kenny Davis backed everyone from Jackie Wilson to Richard Pryor to Marvin Gaye to Lena Horne in venues spanning the Circle Ballroom and the Front Row Theater.

12 OFF TO THE RACES/THE CHASE

A white man and a Black man tell stories about the dangers of performing in Ohio in the late 1950s. One comes from Don George, who as a teenager was the drummer in the Savoys, one of the Cleveland area's earliest rock and roll bands. George would become a major influence in the Cleveland music scene, first as a distributor and wholesaler and later as a promotion man for the Mercury, Casablanca, A&M, IRS, MCA, Polygram, and Interscope labels. The other is from George Hendricks, a Cleveland singer who would star in numerous soul bands of the 1960s and 1970s. At the time of this story, Hendricks was in the Sahibs, a widely admired but sadly unrecorded doo-wop group. Don George died of Covid-19 in February 2021.

According to George, the Savoys recorded in a studio in the basement of the Park Lane Hotel in the University Circle area of Cleveland. They weren't the only musicians to hang there: Eddie Kendricks and Paul Williams, Alabama transplants who would eventually become members of the Temptations, also frequented the studio. The Savoys and those two, who at the time called themselves the Primes, once ended up sharing a marquee. Stella (or Estella or Estelle) "Caldonia" Young, a figure with quite a story of her own, booked the gig, which also featured "Cool Papa" Jarvis, a blues singer.

"This might be '56, '57," George told me in an interview in May 2011. "There was a gal, Estelle Young, a Black woman, ties in with the old prejudice thing. She booked the job in Erie, Pennsylvania. It was a bring-your own-bottle kind of thing, a Black party, a Black dance. She was a shake dancer, a stripper basically. We took two groups in.

"It was on the second floor of a hall, there were windows behind me, and I was the drummer. This is a hot night before air-conditioning. At one point a wine bottle in a brown bag came flying through the window—maybe somebody didn't have the money to pay to get in. The promoter didn't pay us, so I said to Paul Williams, Give me your knife. He said, How you know I have a knife? All you guys carry them, I said. He

laughed and he gave me the knife.

"We took the club's PA system. They had the state police, the local police and the highway patrol—90 wasn't a highway then—all looking for us. I took off with my buddy in his car with the PA equipment and at one point we saw cops coming down the highway with their flashers, so we hid in a cornfield until the cop cars went by. We met over the state line in some truck stop in Ohio and split up and everybody got, like, $2.30 and some cents. We had 17 people. That's all the guy paid us, he gave us like $40, $50, something like that. Stella was in the back seat of my buddy's car. People kind of crammed into the different cars. My buddy had a stand-up bass, he pulled into the parking lot, in another car, he had a '53 Caddy. I didn't even have a license then. All of a sudden this head pops up from under the upright bass, says, That old Mr. Fox didn't catch you boys? That was Stella. She was sitting under there."

Eventually, the owner of the equipment arranged for its return.

"My buddy and I drove the equipment back to Erie, and we met with the guy, a nice guy, who said, I don't know how you guys got out of town; we had everyone looking for you because of the Black situation. Back then, cops were very prejudiced—it was a white world then, you're talking 1957—and that was basically it."

Around that time, the Sahibs played a Black AMVETS hall in a small town south of Streetsboro, Hendricks told me in March 2011. This gig was country.

"We were considered the guys from the big city," Hendricks recalled. "On the way back, coming home from a gig at 1 or 2 o'clock in the morning, if you were Black, you automatically picked up a couple of sheriff's cars." The Sahibs were absolutely that kind of magnet.

"They stopped us, made us get out of the car and searched the car and said, We're going to hold you for investigation. They could hold you for 72 hours then. When we got to the jail, they locked us up, and started asking us where we were coming from that time of the morning, so we told them we were a singing group."

It's one thing to sing for your supper. It's another to sing for your freedom.

"One of the guys said, in a joking way, If you guys are a singing group, come on out here and sing us a song. We did. They let us out of the cells to sing. So after we were done singing, one of the guys—I guess he was trying to be smart—said, I guess we'll let you guys go. We were just glad to get out of there."

13 DON GREGORY

Before I knew the shape *Invisible Soul* would take, I knew its foundation would be the stories of its musicians. One of the ones I approached earliest was Don Gregory, the bass player and leader of Don Gregory and the Montclairs.

Gregory had a local hit in 1965 with "Happy Feet Time," an instrumental on the Sunburst Records label. Sunburst was the brainchild of Jules and Mike Belkin and Carl Maduri, and the single was credited to Belkin-Maduri. I wanted Gregory's story.

In March 2011, I tracked him to his overstuffed, nicotine home in a bombed-out area of East Cleveland. It did not go well. What you're reading is all the Gregory story I have.

Gregory told me if he wrote a biography of Mike Tyson, Tyson would want to be paid for the conversations, so he deserved the same consideration.

Not the same. I wanted to include Gregory in my book, but I wasn't writing his biography; I hoped to write about a scene. The situation at his house on a gloomy, potholed cul-de-sac was saddening and maddening.

I left pissed off. Did Gregory come at me the way he did because he'd been ripped off or because he felt entitled? Whatever the reason, the encounter felt like a loss.

14 RHYMIN' LYMAN

Even though I spent less than a year and a half at Brandeis University—I dropped out with a thud—the place had an impact far above and beyond the academic on me.

Brandeis was where I got high for the first time, at a party a five-minute walk from campus. I barely knew anyone there, but recall it as full of interesting people—including Mel Lyman, a banjo and harmonica wizard in Jim Kweskin & the Jug Band, a joyous aggregation that could be called the original Americana band. Lyman would go on to found Fort Hill Community, a kind of commune, in Roxbury, that eventually spawned the Avatar, a striking and dark underground newspaper. He became a cult figure. He died in 1978 in circumstances that still cry out for clarification and verification.

I only met Lyman that once. He asked me if I wanted to try some "grass." I was curious. He filled his palm with light-green marijuana blades, then rolled them into a joint. He lit it, took a drag, offered it to me, I said OK, and I took my first hit. A sweet, smoky aroma began to haze the room. The next thing I knew, I was by myself, lying on a sofa and listening to Thelonious Monk on the stereo. Be-bop notes danced across the screen behind my eyelids.

How cool.

List of Interviews

FEW OF THE INTERVIEWS at the heart of *Invisible Soul* were more than a single session. Few lasted more than an hour. Hardly any were recorded. Yet after many interviews and many years, they're all memorable in their own way.

They're the yield of countless trips to the inner city of Cleveland, most facilitated by my closest sources for this project, particularly George Hendricks, Harvey Hall and Art Blakey. I approached each subject with a blend of ignorance and open-mindedness, hoping my interviewee would fill in a picture I couldn't predict. My key tool was my laptop: I typed as I queried, realizing in the moment that it might not be the best way to be verifiably accurate, but it remains an essential process of who I am. Along the way, my curiosity led me to unexpected places, and I came away with a deeper understanding of, and affection for, Cleveland.

I cherish those I spoke to for their willingness to shed light on a scene—no, many scenes—too vital to lay to rest. To those who have passed, you are missed.

Freddie Arrington	Kenny Davis	George Hendricks	Walter Ratcliffe
Chuck Avner	Joe DeJarnette	John B. Hicks	Julius Roberts
Eddie Baccus Sr.	Maggie Evans	Bob Holcepl	Eugene Ross
Tom Baker	Jimmy Fox	Ron Iafornaro	Rob Sevier
Larry Banks	Kaye Friedman	Bill Jacocks	David Spero
Michael Bell	Don George	Walter Johnson	Ricky Spicer
Arthur Blakey	Abdul Ghani	Ernie Krivda	Billy Strawbridge
Louise Boddie	Jeff Gould	Hank LoConti	Lee Sykes
Ann Bogan	Leon Green	Joe Lovano	Lynn Tolliver
Alphonso Boyd	Richard Green	Sonny Lovell	Charm Warren
Bill Branch	Travis Haddix	Carl Maduri	Barbara White
Chuck Brown	Harvey Hall	Bobby Massey	James Willis
Eddie Brown	Paul Hamann	"Wild Bill" Matlock	John S. Wilson
Ruthie Brown	Andrew Hamilton	Buddy Maver	Bobby Womack
Carol Browning	Augustus "Gus" Hawkins	Clay Pasternack	Cynthia Woodard
Ray Calabrese	Bobby Harris	Dunn Pearson Jr.	Handy Wright
Phil Coghill	Ken Hawkins	Lou Ragland	J.L. Wright

Mazi's Top Ten CLEVELAND SOUL *Picks*

How could I not be impressed by a guy like Mazi? A cool air about him complements his outsized knowledge of the music he loves. When he first learned about Invisible Soul, he immediately got it: the story, the performers, the music, the audience and especially the vinyl legacy that's so enthralls and immortalizes.

Mazi offers up his top 10 list of the Cleveland Soul-inspired vinyl, including the value, based on his estimate or recent sales. Here's a treasure trove of info on a very visible measure of the treasure of Invisible Soul artifacts.

1 S.O.U.L., *Can You Feel It* Originally released by Musicor Records in 1972. Reissued by Beat Goes Public in 1996. On this second LP by S.O.U.L. (Sounds of Unity and Love), Cleveland native and vocalist, Larry Hancock enters.  With the addition of organ and percussion, I think this LP is superior to S.O.U.L.'s debut album, What Is It. It opens with the feel-good "Can You Feel it?," followed by the Black-conscious message "Tell it Like it is." The first side closes with the heavily sampled funk track "Peace of Mind," made famous by Pete Rock and CL Smooth. Flip to side 2 and the first track is Hancock's version of the Stevie Wonder classic "My Cherie Amour," followed by a psychedelic soul melody entitled "Love, Peace and Power." Track 3 is the quintessential soul ballad, "To Mend a Broken Heart"; both were written and performed by Hancock, and the latter track will make a grown man cry. Gus Hawkins adds the finishing touches with the melancholic "Sleeping Beauty."

$200 (on the low end of things)

2 S.O.U.L., *What is it* Musicor released this in1971, and it was reissued in1994. This psychedelic soul-funk gem was mistakenly named What Is It. Gus Hawkins, the founder of S.O.U.L., told me the group named the LP What it is,  a commonly used phrase (greeting) in the Black community in the early '70's. But this LP was definitely NOT a mistake.

With the emergence of hip hop sampling and the European jazz-dance/ acid jazz scene, Beat Goes Public, a British record label specializing in rare musical gems, reissued What Is It and track 3, "Burning Spear," instantly became a dance floor favorite, with an opening bass line just right for sampling. With an infectious flute solo by Gus Hawkins, it was a must-have for hip hop producers, soul and funk aficionados, as well as record collectors all over.

$300 (if you can find it)

3 Hot Chocolate, *Hot Chocolate*, not to be confused with the British group of the same name. CocoCleveland Records, 1971. All I have to say is "so damn funky." Pure, unadulterated, raw funk. I probably have had more copies of this record than anyone else in the world.

$1,000 (if you are lucky)

4 Lou Ragland, *Lou Ragland Is the Conveyor*, released 1978 on SMH Records. I spent the summer of 1993 in London. I took copies of this album with me on the trip. I could not give them away. A year after my return to Cleveland, I got  a want list from a Japanese collector who offered me $500 for the Lou Ragland Is the Conveyor, the very same LP I struggled to share in England. Funny how things change.

The album opens with the smooth inspirational soul groove track "Understand Each Other." I had the distinct pleasure of meeting him in person at Cleveland's Beachland Ballroom in 2012. In jest, I said, "Well, Lou, you owe your resurrected career to me!"

$500 (could be more)

5 **Pat Stallworth**, *Questions*, Fly- by- Night label, 1974. Starts with a crazy break beat and goes into a mellow grove of female soul.

$400

6 **Creations Unlimited**, *Chrystal Illusion*, Soul Kitchen label, released 1972. This 45 blends rock, rock guitar, and funk grooves and totally makes your head trip. Enough said.

$1,100 (good luck)

7 **Ponderosa Twins + One**, *2+2+1=*, Horoscope Records, 1971. I would be remiss if I did not give a shout out to the Ponderosa Twins +One. It was always a pleasure finding this record. It was Cleveland's own Jackson 5.

$100

8 **Black Unity Trio**, *Al-Fatiah*, Salaam records 1969. This is a record that I discovered. Spiritual free jazz masterpiece.

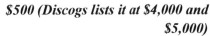

$500 (Discogs lists it at $4,000 and $5,000)

9 **McNeal and Niles**, *Thrust*, Yinkertoo label, 1979. Jazz-fusion-funk classic ripe for sampling. Funky fender Rhodes on "Ja Ja."

10 **Carey Harris and Michael Orr**, *Spread Love*, Sunstar label, 1976. Last, but certainly not least, one of my favorites. The title track has the Gil Scott-Heron space-aged disco spiritual vibe. Recorded at Cleveland's Agency Recording Studio, this is a dance floor classic.

$400

MAZI JAHI: CLEVELAND DJ LEGEND, *record collector, promoter, co-founder of Touch Supper Club, was dubbed "soul archeologist of Cleveland" by American Splendor comic series author and music critic Harvey Pekar. Mazi started his musical journey in the early '90s at the Brillo Pad with an acid jazz night, spinning the rarest, hard-to-find soul, funk, Latin and Brazilian vinyl. His obsession for rare vinyl led Mazi to Africa, Cuba, and Brazil. At Touch Supper Club in the early 2000s, he hosted a weekly event called Salsaturation, featuring Cleveland's finest salsa and Brazilian acts, including Sammy DeLeon, Noel Quintana, Roberto Ocasio, and Moises Borges. Although he no longer hosts events, Mazi enjoys his extensive record collection and the art of the find.*

INSPIRATIONS

The music, its performers and audience were my primary inspirations for this work. Secondary support toward completion of this story comes from a variety of reference media, most of it complete and some that's in process. So many like-minded fans and creators who value the unsung soul stars have inspired me.

I hope Invisible Soul *pays that inspiration forward to drive visibility and credit where it's deserved.*

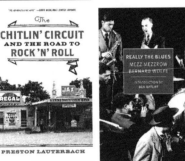

Nowhere To Run:
The Story of Soul Music
by Gerri Hirshey

Published in 1994, not long after soul music peaked, this gripping book is where fans and researchers of that genre must begin.

The Chitlin' Circuit and the Road to Rock 'n' Roll
by Preston Lauterbach

When I reviewed this book in 2011, I called it "a fascinating work about the culture that incubated rock 'n' roll." Cleveland's chitlin' circuit doesn't figure in it. Talk about a vacuum to fill!

Sweet Soul Music: Rhythm and Blues and the Southern Dream of Freedom
by Peter Guralnick

This key work ties the Great Migration to the evolution of Black music. Guralnick is one of the best critics of popular music; his two-volume treatment of Elvis Presley sets the bar for rock biographies, with his bio of Sam Cooke a close second.

Really the Blues
by Mezz Mezzrow and Bernard Wolfe
Like Invisible Soul

At its foundation, this is an oral history of jazz and race from nearly 100 years

ago, It's profoundly counter-cultural and memorable. I continue to think about it years after first reading it.

What It Is! Funky Soul and Rare Grooves 1967-1977
This Rhino Records anthology presents 91 tracks, many of them B-sides. It captures the period effectively, and its diversity is encouraging. Great liner notes and packaging, too. And unlike a S.O.U.L. album of nearly the same name, it gets its title right.

Boddi Recording CD Set
By Numero Group
This Chicago-based archival record company effectively got the Invisible Soul ball rolling in 2011 when it released its three-CD Boddie Recording Company set. Numero's curiosity, research prowess and the way it honors unjustly overlooked music work together just right.

Soul Music of Ohio
by Dante Carfagna

Carfagna has worked with Numero Group for years, collects and chronicles rare soul records. And collect he does. This 344-page volume showcases over 1,700 artists, 500 record companies, and 3,000 individual releases. The numbers don't lie, but they do impress. Wow.

Summer of Soul

Last year, we were fortunate enough to be invited to the Rock and Roll Hall of Fame for the premiere of Questlove's Oscar-winning documentary of a summer concert series in the Bronx. For a good 50 years, high quality, multi-camera recordings of these free concerts in 1969 languished, unwatched, in a storage locker. Any fan of music needs to spend 90 minutes basking in the Summer of Soul.

Mind Over Matter: The Myths and Mysteries of Detroit's Fortune Records, by Billy Miller and Michel Hurtt

Ridiculously researched, gorgeously illustrated and defiantly heavy, this is a must buy for the soul geek. In granular detail, we learn the story of a definitively mom-and-pop label that turned out great soul, rhythm and blues and country records, including the divine doo-wop of Nolan Strong and the Diablos. Getting this material to market, in the shadow of Motown, was another matter. I prize my Fortune bootleg CDs.

Music & Entertainment Memories of Black Cleveland

by LaMont Showboat Robinson, with illustrator Russell LiquidRaw Johnson and a foreword by John "Sly" Wilson.

This is a memorabilia-studded diary of the entertainment scene of Black Cleveland between the mid-1940s and the 1970s. It's a picture book, packed with reproductions of vintage newspaper ads and show bills. Robinson is founder and CEO of the National Rhythm & Blues Hall of Fame, formed in 2010. Currently the hall is largely virtual, with plans for a bricks-and-mortar iteration to open in 2024 in Marks, Mississippi.

Soul City Cleveland

This highly anticipated documentary by Fanon Hill is said to feature interviews and highlights of the stars that made Cleveland's soul scene shine. Can't wait for a screening.

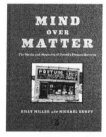

ACKNOWLEDGMENTS

THIS BOOK TOOK A GOOD 12 YEARS FROM conception to execution. It started as a Facebook page, which still exists. Over time, it became more ambitious, complicated and personal. There were times I feared it would never end, but here we are. I hope it's an enjoyable, informative and thought-provoking read. Maybe even a change agent.

I couldn't have produced *Invisible Soul* without Act3creative, my publisher since 2016. I particularly thank James O'Hare, my writing partner, editor and sounding board, for his enthusiasm, encouragement, and curiosity re: *Invisible Soul*, not to mention his knowledge of and love for his native Cleveland. Jim "got it" when I wasn't sure I did, and he persevered, deepening it at every turn. Ron Hill "got" the look for *Invisible Soul* with his imaginative illustrations, no mean trick considering how so much of that scene is gone. Jaime Lombardo's inspired cover design makes *Invisible Soul* visible. Graphic designer Michael Schwartz poured the text into the right format; looking good, Michael.

I also want to thank the following for the many conversations we had about this book over the years:

Eric Lazarus, one of my oldest friends, for his support, advice, and profound insight into a very complex process. Writing this engrossed me even as it took me way out of my comfort zone. My Skypes with Eric, with me in Cleveland, him in Burlington, Vermont, kept me on track.

Mark David Ribbins, the Jazz Preacher of Cleveland, for his glowing Foreword and for being a friend for the long haul.

The fine Cleveland artist Matt Sweeney for keeping me honest by asking me, Do you really want to finish this? Do you really want to let it go? Read the book, Matt.

The Cleveland Afrofururist RA Washington for his penetrating commentary on this book's tone and intent (thanks, Chuck Mintz).

My cousin Peter Wolff, for our Google Meets about the book you're now holding and Peter's *I Am the Water*, a memoir he's been working on for several years. Peter, who lives in Berlin, is a life coach and a very wise man.

I could not have done this without the support of my wife **Karen Sandstrom**, a wonderfully ruthless editor, a fabulous illustrator, and a writer so good she continues to be my role model.

I also want to thank **Ivan Sheehan** and his long-defunct website **ohioauthority.com** for publishing early Invisible Soul pieces. I want to credit the **Rock and Roll Hall of Fame** for presenting me and Lou Ragland in 2013.

Early versions of material on Motown and 105 were published in **Great Lakes Review** in 2012 and 2013.

Eric and Dawn Olsen, for conversations about how hard and rewarding it is to build a book.

Mike Butz, for his rigorous insights and editing acumen.

Alex Vicarel, for our many discovery sessions, smart edits and on-target questions from a young writer.

ABOUT

CARLO WOLFF writes about popular culture, music, books, hospitality and travel. A contributor to the jazz magazine, DownBeat, he is the author of *Cleveland Rock & Roll Memories*, lead author of *Mike Belkin: Socks, Sports, Rock and Art*, and co-writer of *Designing Victory* and *The Encyclopedia of Record Producers*. Wolff also reports and edits for newspapers and magazines. A native of Dallas, Wolff grew up in Columbus, Ohio and attended schools in the Boston area. He moved to Cleveland in 1986. Wolff lives in Cleveland with his wife Karen Sandstrom and Daisy the Dog.

JAMES O'HARE is a multi-modal media producer. O'Hare's background in editing, corporate branding, and communications technology is key to bringing new approaches to storytellers and audiences. A lifelong Cleveland area resident, Jim lives in Cleveland Heights with his wife, Joyce.

RON HILL is a cartoonist, illustrator, caricature artist, creative director, author, editor and educator. Since 1999, he has created weekly editorial cartoons for four award-winning Cleveland-area weekly newspapers. In 2008, his work earned a Cleveland Press Club award for Best Editorial Cartoon in Ohio. He is a member of the American Association of Editorial Cartoonists.

Invisible Soul's Facebook page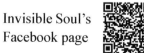